Frenchtown Chronicles of Prairie du Chien

-Introduction-

This is a short sketch of the truthful incidents of the life of Julian Coryer. written by his grandson Albert Coryer

This was truthfully told by Julian himself to his wife Lucretia and his son Joseph which was handed down to Albert the writer.

Now as to the name Coryer. This not the correct spelling or pronounciation of this name. The correct or incorrect French name and spelling of it is Carraire. The change took place at the Crawford Co Court house it was changed gradually through land transactions and tax receipts There is a special certificate on file in the Crawford County records telling how and when the changes took place.

MARY ELISE ANTOINE

FRENCHTOWN CHRONICLES OF PRAIRIE DU CHIEN

*History and Folklore from
Wisconsin's Frontier*

EDITED BY MARY ELISE ANTOINE
AND LUCY ELDERSVELD MURPHY

WISCONSIN HISTORICAL SOCIETY PRESS

Published by the Wisconsin Historical Society Press
Publishers since 1855

The Wisconsin Historical Society helps people connect to the past
by collecting, preserving, and sharing stories. Founded in 1846,
the Society is one of the nation's finest historical institutions.

Order books by phone toll free: (888) 999-1669
Order books online: shop.wisconsinhistory.org
Join the Wisconsin Historical Society: wisconsinhistory.org/membership

Photographs identified with WHi or WHS are from the Society's collections; address requests to reproduce these photos to the Visual Materials Archivist at the Wisconsin Historical Society, 816 State Street, Madison, WI 53706.

Cover image: George Catlin painting *Prairie du Chien, United States Garrison*, Smithsonian American Art Museum, Gift of Mrs. Joseph Harrison Jr.

Printed in Canada
Designed by Ryan Scheife / Mayfly Design

20 19 18 17 16   1 2 3 4 5

Library of Congress Cataloging-in-Publication Data

Names: Coryer, Albert, 1877-1968. | Antoine, Mary Elise. | Murphy, Lucy
   Eldersveld, 1953-
Title: Frenchtown chronicles of Prairie du Chien : history and folklore from
   Wisconsin's frontier / edited by Mary Elise Antoine and Lucy Eldersveld
   Murphy.
Description: Madison, WI : Wisconsin Historical Society Press, 2016. |
   Includes bibliographical references and index.
Identifiers: LCCN 2016003033| ISBN 9780870207594 (hardcover : alkaline paper)
   | ISBN 9780870207600 (ebook)
Subjects: LCSH: Prairie du Chien (Wis.) —History—Anecdotes. | Frenchtown
   (Prairie du Chien, Wis.) —History—Anecdotes. | Prairie du Chien
   (Wis.) —Social life and customs—Anecdotes. | Prairie du Chien
   (Wis.) —Ethnic relations—History—Anecdotes. | Frontier and pioneer
   life—Wisconsin—Prairie du Chien—Anecdotes. | Farm
   life—Wisconsin—Prairie du Chien—History—Anecdotes. | Prairie du Chien
   (Wis.) —Biography—Anecdotes. | Coryer, Albert, 1877-1968—Family. |
   Coryer, Albert, 1877-1968—Interviews. | Folklore—Wisconsin—Prairie du
   Chien.
Classification: LCC F589.P8 C67 2016 | DDC 977.5/74—dc23 LC record available at https://lccn
   .loc.gov/2016003033

♾ The paper used in this publication meets the minimum requirements of the American National Standard for Information Sciences—Permanence of Paper for Printed Library Materials, ANSI Z39.48-1992.

CONTENTS

Introduction

Albert Coryer loved to tell stories. The grandson of a nineteenth-century voyageur, he grew up hearing tales about his grandfather's adventures in the fur trade on the Mississippi and Missouri Rivers, and he passed them on to friends and family. During his boyhood, Albert lived on the family farm, learning about the land and the people who lived in Prairie du Chien's Frenchtown neighborhood. After he left the farm and moved into the city of Prairie du Chien, he worked as a school janitor, marrying only late in life. As he grew older, Coryer became known as a talented storyteller, spinning tales of his and his family members' experiences to audiences that included his younger relatives, his neighbors, and his friends. Eventually, he started to put these stories to paper. He spent many hours filling up dime-store writing tablets with handwritten anecdotes and reminiscences that he had told many times before. In his early seventies, he drew a detailed illustrated map, eight by twenty-eight inches in size, showing what Frenchtown had been like around 1860, based on the stories he had heard. Another map attributed to Albert was even larger and more detailed. By 1951, when he had outlived most of his contemporaries and had gained a reputation for his storytelling ability and knowledge of Prairie du Chien history, a local historian interviewed him. This volume brings together Albert Coryer's written stories and oral interview, along with the rich visual representation provided by his map.

Taken together, these narratives provide a unique, multifaceted view of Prairie du Chien's late-nineteenth-century rural outskirts and Frenchtown neighborhood—its people, physical landscape, economy, and French-Canadian and Creole culture.* Albert Coryer had a keen sense of geography and the history of the natural world, the people who lived on the land along the river and the ways they interacted. In addition, his memory saved the tales of his voyageur grandfather—embellishing some

---

*The term Creole refers to people whose culture predates the arrival of the United States to this region, and who had European ancestry—usually French-Canadian, sometimes mixed with Native. Generally Creoles were born in North America, not in Europe, and frequently they were born in the Great Lakes region.

of them, inventing others. This book is thus oral history, folklore, memoir, and myth.

Albert Coryer was the eldest child of Joseph and Malvina Langford Coryer. His paternal grandparents had come to Prairie du Chien as a young couple. Grandfather Julian Carriere had been born in a small village along the south bank of the St. Lawrence River, southeast of Montreal. As a young man, he engaged to work in the Missouri fur trade. For a few years, Julian lived in St. Louis, where he met and married Lucretia Lessard (also known as Leocadie) in 1836. Julian and Lucretia had only one child, Joseph, born in 1845 in Prairie du Chien. At the age of nineteen, Joseph married Malvina, the eldest child of Thaddeus and Eliza Langford. Joseph and Malvina had three children: Albert Eugene, Idella M. (known as Della), and George Elmer. As the years passed, the pronunciation and spelling of the family name Carriere slowly changed. By 1900, the family was using the anglicized version: Coryer. While public documents list his first name as Julien, Albert referred to his grandfather as Julian, so that spelling is used throughout this text.

As a young boy, Albert grew up in a very close, tight-knit community, which the residents of Prairie du Chien called "Frenchtown." Born on August 31, 1877, he lived for forty-five years on the land his grandfather Julian had purchased in Limery Coulee, a ravine that led from the prairie to the bluffs overlooking the community. In the first years of Albert's life, his grandfather Julian and grandmother Lucretia lived with Joseph and Malvina, so three generations comprised the household. Lucretia's brothers, Jean Baptiste and Joseph Lessard, had also purchased land in Limery Coulee, as had François Gauthier (later known as Francis Gokey), who had married Marie Anne, Lucretia's sister. The Lessard and Gokey farms were worked by the couples and their children. As Albert grew up, his relatives lived only a short walk away. Many evenings after the cows had been milked and the animals fed, Albert and his family and relatives often gathered in one of the homes. After an exchange of news and gossip, someone would start telling stories. Many of the stories would be about the "old days" when Julian, Francis, and Jean Baptiste had been young men and had sought adventure far from home. Albert may have heard Julian himself relate his adventures, but Julian died when Albert was only five. Even after Julian's death, the stories of hardships and exploits in the

This Coryer family portrait was taken circa 1900–1910. Standing are Albert Coryer, Della Coryer, and George Coryer. Seated are Joseph Coryer and Malvina Langford Coryer.
CORYER FAMILY

Missouri fur trade, the long journey to the California goldfields, and other recollections of Julian's family continued to be told and retold.

Albert received a basic education in the Frenchtown School, a one-room structure where children of all ages received instruction. Albert later recalled his schoolmates, who included not only his sister and brother but also Langford and Gokey cousins. They were joined by children of other families who lived in Frenchtown, some of French-Canadian ancestry, others whose grandparents and parents had emigrated from Germany. Education continued to be important to Albert as an adult. He went on to serve as a board member and treasurer for Frenchtown School District #9 in Prairie du Chien Township.

Hearing the stories of his grandfather and his great-uncle, Albert longed to travel, even wishing to enlist to fight in the Spanish-American War. But Albert's father, Joseph, had lost his health and could not work the farm, so, heeding the wishes of his mother, Albert stayed at home to help his father on the farm. But the desire to travel persisted, and in 1910 Albert left Prairie du Chien for the West, convincing his family to join him. In the fall of that year, Albert and Della each purchased 160 acres near Galatea in Kiowa County, Colorado; Joseph purchased 152 acres. For three years, they homesteaded, but the hardships became too great. They left for San Diego, California, where his brother George resided. Albert and George were employed as laborers, assisting in the construction of buildings for the Panama-California Exposition. When Joseph Coryer died on October 1, 1913, they all returned to Prairie du Chien for the burial. In January 1914, their sister Della married Edward Leamy. Della and Edward lived on the Coryer farm for a few years with George, Malvina, and Albert, who had decided to return to farming in Limery Coulee. When the draft law of August 1918 required that all men from ages eighteen to forty-five register for military service, Albert complied. After the family sold the farm in Limery Coulee, Albert worked for a while at the woolen mill in Prairie du Chien, was employed at the J. I. Case Company in Racine, Wisconsin, and tried his hand at clamming. But adventure still called, so he began to travel again. He sold the land in Colorado and moved to Omaha, Nebraska, spending the winters picking oranges in Florida. On his way back to Prairie du Chien, Albert spent a year building bridges in Iowa.

Albert E. Coryer and Mary Veronica Welch were married June 12, 1954. DONNA A. HIGGINS

His wanderlust fulfilled, Albert settled down. With the farm sold, Albert and his mother lived in a house on North Michigan Street, and Edward and Della Leamy moved in next door. After Malvina died in 1931, Albert lived with the Leamy family for several years. In 1935, Albert began to work at Campion Jesuit High School in Prairie du Chien. Initially, he worked in the kitchen and dining hall for six years and then as a janitor for the next thirty-four years. In 1954, at the age of seventy-six, Albert married Mary Veronica Welch. She was known as Vera. They lived in a house on North Beaumont Road. In 1965, at the age of eighty-eight, Albert retired from Campion. Three years later, he died at the age of ninety in February 1968. He was buried in Calvary Cemetery next to his grandparents and parents.

PRAIRIE DU CHIEN

The stories Albert recorded are part of the long and rich history of the community that was his lifetime home. Prairie du Chien was the name given to the prairie that lay north of the confluence of the Wisconsin and Mississippi Rivers. Ancient Indian mounds testify that Native people have lived, farmed, and traded here for many centuries. The prairie had been a gathering place for the Native people of the upper Mississippi long before the arrival of the first Euro-Americans at the end of the seventeenth century. French fur-trader explorers soon followed the Fox-Wisconsin water route taken by Jacques Marquette and Louis Jolliet in 1673, but many, upon arriving at the Mississippi River, turned their canoes north. The Frenchmen found the prairie to be a perfect site to stop, rest, and meet and trade with the Indians who used the prairie as a neutral gathering place. During the late seventeenth and mid-eighteenth centuries, Frenchmen Nicolas Perrot and Joseph Marin constructed seasonal fortifications for the French fur trade on the prairie and the banks of the upper Mississippi.

In 1737, after a quarter century of violence between the French and Meskwakis known as the Fox Wars, Meskwaki Indians built a village here and devoted their energies to building up commerce as a way to achieve peace and rebuild their economy.[1] But the Fox Wars, and the French and Indian War between France and Great Britain at midcentury, kept any European settlement from occurring on the prairie. After the end of the war, the western Great Lakes–upper Mississippi fur trade passed into the hands of British-Canadians. French-Canadian men continued to be part of the fur trade and seasonally visited the prairie, many of them marrying into the local tribes and creating culturally mixed families. They established wintering sites in the upper Mississippi close to the Native villages and campsites to exchange European goods for furs and other Indian products.

Because Prairie du Chien was considered a neutral gathering area as well as an important site of the yearly rendezvous, increasing numbers of fur traders and their employees, many of whom had married into the tribes with which they traded, took up residence on the prairie in the last quarter of the eighteenth century. Prairie du Chien served a fur trade region that included not only Meskwaki (also known as Fox) Indians but also the Sauk, Ho-Chunk, Dakota, Menominee, Potawatomi, and Ojibwe. By the 1780s, the mixed French-Indian families were joined by a few French-speaking men and families from the Illinois Country. In 1781 the British government formally purchased the land from the Meskwaki. By the end of the eighteenth century more migrants arrived from Canada, both French- and British-Canadians. These men were traders and voyageurs, and they often married Indian women of the upper Mississippi Valley, where the Canadians traded. As the Illinois French and then Canadians arrived at Prairie du Chien, each selected land for their homes, for their trading houses, and for cultivation. By 1800, much of the prairie land had been partitioned.

By 1810, three small villages existed at Prairie du Chien, containing about three hundred residents during the summer months. On a large island just west of the prairie was the Main Village. Here, the traders lived and conducted the fur trade of the upper Mississippi River and its tributaries. On the prairie, separated from the Main Village by a slough (that is, a marshy area or *marais*), stood the Village of St. Friol. To the north, along an old Indian trail, lay the Upper Village. The rest of the prairie was divided into long lots where cattle and horses grazed in common, and residents tended their personal fields.

By the time the United States gained control of the region after the War of 1812, about six hundred members of fur-trade families had made Prairie du Chien their home, and the Meskwakis moved their village to the south.[2] There were many other similar fur trade communities around the Great Lakes region in the early nineteenth century, including Green Bay, Michilimackinac, Detroit, St. Louis, and Vincennes.[3]

Some controversy exists about the origin of the town's name. Visitor Jonathan Carver in 1766 recorded the name of the place as La Prairie le Chien.[4] According to an early resident it became known as the home of a large Native family called *Des Chiens*, the dogs. When Lt. Zebulon Pike visited the prairie in September 1805 as part of his exploration of the upper Mississippi for the United States, he learned that the prairie "derived its name from a family of Reynards [Meskwaki] who formerly lived there, distinguished by the appellation of Dogs."[5]

In the summer of 1829, Julian Carriere saw Prairie du Chien for the first time. He and fellow voyageurs, on their journey from Quebec to St. Louis, stopped at Prairie du Chien to deliver messages and pick up information for transportation to St. Louis. Albert later recalled that his grandfather stated that he saw the trading houses "located along the river bank" in the Main Village. Besides the fur traders, Albert remembered Julian saying that there were "a few settlers along the east side of the slough." These would be the people who lived in the other two villages. Though his grandson does not mention it, Julian probably also saw the old log Fort Crawford that stood behind the houses in the Main Village and the stone barracks being constructed on the prairie to the south for the new Fort Crawford, one of a chain of forts that stretched from the foot of Lake Michigan to the Falls of St. Anthony at present-day St. Paul.

Albert Coryer's family began to put down roots in Prairie du Chien in about 1840, when his great-uncles Jean Baptiste and François Lessard came to Prairie du Chien on a business trip, selling horses. They loved the beautiful town and its surrounding area and decided to settle there. Soon they convinced their sister Lucretia and her husband, Julian, to join them. Eventually, in a typical chain migration, their brother Joseph, sister Marie Anne, and mother, Marie Rose, joined the family there.[6]

By the time Julian and Lucretia arrived in Prairie du Chien to settle alongside relatives, the community was undergoing great changes and losing much of its French character. Speculators were purchasing property and forming land companies. The farm lots were surveyed and partitioned into blocks and lots and offered for sale. The log houses built by Frenchmen in the villages were being torn down to be replaced by commercial structures.

While French Canadians such as the Lessards and other fur-trade family members were moving to Prairie du Chien, increasing numbers of English-speaking settlers from New England, New York, and other points east were moving to Prairie du Chien. By 1836, these newcomers numerically overwhelmed the French-speaking residents. The fur trade went into decline as the United States signed treaties with the Indian nations and forced them to give up their homelands and move west to reservations. The residents of Prairie du Chien who had made the community their home and found livelihood in the fur trade had to decide whether to move to the northwest to follow the trade, or to stay and adapt to changing economic realities. Many, including the Lessards and Coryers, chose to stay and make their living from the land by farming and other subsistence activities, such as fishing and hunting.[7] Albert Coryer's stories help us to understand the patterns of life lived on the land.

The departing fur trade significantly altered the local economy. Many French-speaking residents decided to leave Prairie du Chien and follow the fur trade as it moved north and west. As they left, they began to sell or abandon the land they had farmed at Prairie du Chien. Speculators from the eastern United States, especially New York, saw the value of the farmland at Prairie du Chien. Beginning in the 1830s, speculators bought up the farms on the southern end of the prairie, surveying them into blocks and lots. With the arrival of the Milwaukee and Mississippi Railroad in 1857, the southern end of Prairie du Chien grew. Fort Crawford had been closed by the US Army the year before, making more land available. This commercial and residential growth moved north. The old Main Village and the Village of St. Friol were swallowed up by manufacturing concerns. New businesses opened as immigrants from Ireland, Germany, and Bohemia made Prairie du Chien their home.

To the newcomers, the two cemeteries established many years before on the northern fringe of the Village of St. Friol seemed to stand as an obstacle to the expansion and construction. When the City of Prairie du Chien was incorporated in 1872, the northern boundary of the municipality was drawn just south of the cemeteries. Separated from the city, the prairie north of Calvary Cemetery and the old French Cemetery saw its life and traditions altered little. For example, the Grimard, Chenevert, L'Emerie, and Cherrier families, who had come to the prairie years before for the fur trade but had turned to farming the northern part of the prairie, continued to live on and farm the land of their ancestors.

From the 1830s to 1850s, thousands of French-speaking people left their homes in Lower Canada. Some followed the rivers into New England. Others were drawn westward to where voyageurs had paddled the upper Mississippi. The Mississippi River and Prairie du Chien drew many of these French-Canadians, some in family groups and others as individuals who later married into the local community. As they had been farmers in Canada, most wanted to continue farming. Many settled on the north end of the prairie at Prairie du Chien, feeling a comfortable sense of home with the old French families who resided there. This sense of familiarity is what drew Julian and Lucretia Carriere to settle at Prairie du Chien and on the north end of the prairie. Not only were the Lessard and Gauthier relatives living here, but other families from the same background also had their homes in the old village.

The people who lived and worked on Bluff, Church, Minnesota, and Michigan Streets in the city looked north and saw themselves as separate and different from those people who spoke French among themselves. All might see each other every Sunday at St. Gabriel's Church, but after Mass the "Frenchmen" turned their wagons into the ruts of the old Indian trail and headed north. The rest of the congregation turned south and walked to their homes. Little by little, the old Indian trail came to be called "Frenchtown Road." The community that spread along the road and east to the bluffs became known as "Frenchtown." Albert Coryer's map and many of his stories focus on this Frenchtown neighborhood.

ALBERT CORYER AS STORYTELLER

Albert Coryer had a wonderfully retentive memory. He remembered stories that he had heard as a young boy and told the same stories to his nieces and nephews, and later to his great niece and great nephew. According to Susan Leamy Kies, his great niece, Albert "loved to reminisce about the old days. His hand movements were as much a part of his tales as his words, rising and falling with the action, resting on his knees during the dramatic interludes. He spoke slowly and deliberately, the words carefully chosen to emote the desired tone." Also included in his recollections were tales his mother had related about her father, Thaddeus. Eventually Albert decided to write down the stories he had heard and continued to relate about his two grandfathers, Julian Carriere and Thaddeus Wright Langford. And so Albert began to record what he remembered of the stories he had heard as a young boy about his family and about life in "Frenchtown" long ago.

Coryer's stories, no doubt, had been told many times. His descriptions of the people, and his drawings of their activities, give a sense that he had considered them often, and that they had been discussed in groups of old-timers sitting around their favorite gathering place. It is likely that Coryer presents a kind of collective community memory of the "old French people," as he called Prairie du Chien's French-Creole settlers. Certainly nostalgia colored the memories, and there is in addition a sense of personal involvement with the events and society as Coryer tried to depict the culture and values—as well as the characters and incidents—in the lives of his parents and grandparents and their neighbors. Since Coryer's mother came from an English-speaking family, his English was good, and he had multiple perspectives of the past, but he seems to have identified primarily with the "French" population in depicting this community.

He continued this identity long after the death of his grandparents and parents. When members of the extended Gokey family and their many relatives gathered in a home, Albert was invited to join. After the meal, he was one of the men who led the singing of the songs sung by voyageurs as they paddled the large canoes on the waters leading from Montreal to Prairie du Chien. When the dancing started, he clapped in time to the fiddling of French-Canadian tunes.[8]

Albert Coryer's narratives and maps emphasize topics of particular interest to him, and those he thought his listeners and readers wanted to know about. Above all, he sketched a community in which French-Creole values emphasized family, friendship, community, mutual aid, resourcefulness, and humor. He depicted a world where Indians were still present (if marginal), even though most of the tribes had been removed. His depictions of the influential Dousman and Rolette families are respectful on the surface, but if we look closely, we detect a certain glee on the author's part at the ways in which ordinary people subverted the well-to-do people's efforts to control most of the natural resources. We note his pride and pleasure in telling stories about successful Native and French-Canadian healers who used specialized knowledge, herbal medicines, and a specific faith-based set of prayers and practices to cure the sick and injured who had been given up and despaired of by the medical doctors of the time.

Central to the characters of Albert's stories were their efforts as farmers. He discussed the livestock they raised, the crops, the housing they built themselves. Hogs and horses could be allowed to roam in common areas. The natural world was also central to these stories and his map. Residents supplemented their farm income by selling firewood, hunting, and fishing. We learn where the creeks and rivers were, what fish swam there, and the different ways that Indian and non-Indian people fished. The map shows the townspeople with their wagons and rowboats, their houses, wells, orchards, and the local Indian mounds. He located the school, the first bowling alley, and the first brick building, and he depicted residents harvesting wild hay on an island. Albert's stories also show an awareness of ecological change in the extinction of passenger pigeons, the ways that prairies were affected when settlers stopped burning the grasses, and the ways that creeks silted up.

About the Text

Our intention has been to provide a collection of these unique stories and colorful reminiscences to entertain and inform readers who have an interest in local, regional, ethnic, and frontier history and folklore. We have been able to locate five separate texts created by Albert Coryer, all handwritten: a collection called "Short Stories Handed Down . . .," "A true Ghost Story," "The Grandson of Two Runaway Granddads," "The Life of Julian Coryer," and "A short sketch of truthful incidents in the life of Julian Coryer . . ." To avoid confusion between these last two, the latter will be referred to in this book as "the Bittner voyageur manuscript," because Albert gave the manuscript to Florence Bittner. A transcript of an interview with Albert by Florence Bittner, former curator of the Villa Louis historic site in Prairie du Chien, provides additional stories and details. The interview transcript and a copy of "Short Stories Handed Down" are located at the Wisconsin Historical Society, while the original "Short Stories Handed Down" and other four manuscripts are privately owned and used with permission. We have also included two delightful illustrated maps of Frenchtown, which include references to stories Albert told in the interview.

In editing the manuscripts, we have tried to maintain Coryer's style and voice while polishing the texts just enough to make them clear for readers. We corrected Coryer's spelling, capitalization, punctuation, and paragraph breaks. Where he used abbreviations, we spelled the words out. In the interview transcripts, where Coryer stammered, saying a word twice, we deleted the repeated word. Many of his sentences began with the word "and," which we deleted in many instances. When he said "'em" instead of "them," we corrected the transcript. In some cases we corrected his grammar by inserting the correct verbs into the text in brackets. In addition, because Coryer seemed not to have realized that the word "squaw" is a pejorative, hurtful term, we substituted another word such as "woman" in its stead, in brackets.

Coryer titled many of his own stories, and these titles have been preserved. Where a story lacked a title, we have supplied one, italicizing it to differentiate it from Coryer's own.

Some of Coryer's stories appeared in more than one of the texts, and in the editing process, we selected one version but added sentences from the other manuscripts, indicating in the endnotes the source of the added material. The materials are organized by topic, covering rural life in the 1800s, the people and culture of Prairie du Chien, the experiences of the voyageurs in the Missouri River fur trade, and several stories about the supernatural beliefs of the time. We hope that readers will enjoy Albert's stories and maps, and also gain from them a better understanding of the people, community, lifeways, and culture of this very important old fur-trade community.

PART 1

RURAL LIFE

In recording the short stories of nineteenth-century rural life that were handed down to him by his parents and grandparents, Albert Coryer commented extensively on the land and waterways and their creatures. He described the ecosystems and the ways they were changed by human residents. The stories express his keen awareness of—and concern for—the region's wildlife, and his knowledge about the ways that his family and neighbors interacted with the natural world.

In some stories, Coryer focused on farm life, explaining in detail how families such as his grew and harvested grain; raised livestock; and preserved fruit, butter, and other products for their own use and for market. These accounts depict a local economy in which subsistence activities such as hunting, fishing, and woodcutting supplemented farmwork by providing both food for the dining table and products such as hoop poles for barrels or firewood to sell.

As in many early communities, the residents of Prairie du Chien had long considered much of the land and river areas to be commons, that is, resources available to be used by anyone. As individuals and their families carved out and claimed specific parcels of land, the commons were diminished. At times the parceling of land led to conflicts, as in the 1820s, when some settlers claimed land their neighbors thought should remain communal. Still, for a long time residents could let their cattle, horses, and hogs range freely while residents fenced in their gardens and fields to protect them. In the late nineteenth century, landowners started fencing in the livestock instead.

A few residents built their wealth by acquiring a great deal of real estate. One of the most successful was the fur trader Hercules L. Dousman, who looms large in Coryer's narrative. Dousman's family and their mansion became a focal point of Prairie du Chien history during Coryer's lifetime, and later the historic site provided employment for local historians such as Florence Bittner, whose interview with Coryer appears in sections here and later in this volume. Although Bittner expected—and it was customary for—local histories to portray Hercules L. Dousman in a

Albert Coryer with his team and rig at the top of Limery Coulee. CORYER FAMILY

positive light, Coryer's stories expressed considerable ambivalence about Dousman. In particular, Dousman was depicted as a man who tried to steal Albert's grandparents' farm until threatened by his outraged grandfather, and as a man who only begrudgingly shared the resources of wild lands he had claimed with local children and less-wealthy farmers. The reader can detect Coryer's sense of triumph when young fishermen or local wood-cutters went home with resources that Dousman had considered his own. In Coryer's tales, local farm families as well as Indians seem to have had less deference for Dousman than one might expect.

Indian people figure prominently in these stories, beginning with the very first tale. Did Coryer begin with it because it was his favorite? No doubt he knew that his audiences would be interested in hearing about the frontier days before Indian removal, when Native people commonly lived nearby and interacted with the non-Native residents. It may have surprised as well as comforted his readers and listeners to hear about the relatively peaceful relations between settlers and Indians in the 1800s, in contrast to the violent encounters and more racist depictions that were popular in movies and fiction when Coryer was sharing these stories during the mid-twentieth century. Notably, Coryer refers to members of all different tribes using the generic term "Indians." He did not seem to

make a distinction between specific tribes or bands of Ho-Chunk, Meskwaki, Sauk, or Dakota. Nor did he seem to know any individual Native
people himself.

Coryer's stories cover mostly friendly interactions between settlers
and Indians, with the exchange of aid, hospitality, gifts of food and trin-
kets, healing assistance, and knowledge. He seems to depict a world in
which settlers feared wolves and robbers more than Native people. Yet
careful examination paints a less harmonious picture. Coryer describes
a place where only remnants of Indian cornfields remain, where a young
girl is taken from a Native family she longs for, and where intermarriage
between Native and non-Native people is increasingly rare. These repre-
sent mere hints of the larger picture of what was happening to American
Indians during Coryer's lifetime. The US government forced the local
tribes of Ho-Chunk, Sauk, Meskwaki, and Dakota to remove north and
west in the mid-nineteenth century. Some of the intermarried Native
people and their relatives who had kin among the settlers were able to stay,
as were some tribes located in the north and east such as the Ojibwe and
Menominee. Some Ho-Chunk fled when they reached undesirable new
reservations in the west, surreptitiously returning to Wisconsin. But Native people were increasingly marginalized: while Joseph Drew and Julian
Carriere spoke Native languages, Albert Coryer apparently did not. Coryer's more limited awareness of American Indians may have influenced the
way he wrote about them. While the characters he writes possess positive
traits, they seem to rely more on stereotypes than cultural understanding.
Coryer focused more on the ways they helped and interacted with their
white neighbors than on their own diverse cultures and histories.

While most of the stories that follow come from Coryer's "Short Stories
Handed Down . . . ," several related excerpts from the Bittner interview and
other manuscripts also have been included, as noted.

Short Stories Handed Down to Me, Albert Coryer, by My Parents and Grandparents, Mr. and Mrs. Julian Coryer and Mr. and Mrs. Thaddeus Langford

Julian Coryer came from Canada at the age of sixteen. He was born in 1813. He first saw Prairie du Chien in 1829. Prairie du Chien was then a fur trading post along the riverbank and others lived as farmers. They lived along what was then known as the Indian trail which is now known as Main Street in the city limits and continues north, which was known as Frenchtown which . . . extended north to the Mill coulee [ravine] at that time. This coulee was known as Fisher Creek; a large creek flowed here which was fed by springs which gushed out of the hillsides. Speckled trout was plentiful in those creeks.

Then later a Mr. William Mosier built a flour mill about one-half mile from the mouth of this coulee.[1] He used water for power by forming a dam and mill run. . . . This coulee was then called Mill Coulee. The first flour mill was built in Frenchtown; it was built entirely of wood except the two large round and flat stones. The wheat and corn [were] ground by passing through the two stones. This mill was operated with a tread power. Oxen were used to tread the power. Cornmeal and graham flour [were] all that could be ground in this mill: there were no sieves to separate the white from the bran.

The Gays put the first flour mill in Crawford County that produced white flour. This mill was built and operated with water from the Kickapoo River. This was the start of the village of Gays Mills. This mill was built about the year 1840. Waterpower was the cheapest power at that time: a large waterwheel was the only material used to produce the power.

Short stories handed down to me, Albert Coryer, by my parents and Grand parents Mr. & Mrs. Julian Coryer, and Mr. and Mrs. Thaddeus Langford.

Julian Coryer came from Canada at the age of 16 he was born in 1813 thereby he first saw Prairie du Chien in 1829.

Prairie du Chien was then a fur trading post along the river bank and others lived as farmers (they lived) along what was then known as the Indian trail which is now known as Main street in the city limits and continues north which was known as Frenchtown which it extended north to the Mill coulee at that time. This coulee was known as Fischer creek a large creek flowed here which was fed by springs which gushed out of the hill sides. Speckled trout was plentiful in those creeks.

Then later a Mr. Wm. Woshier built a flour mill about ½ mile from the mouth of this coulee he used water for power by forming a dam and a mill race to the mill. This coulee was then called Mill Coulee

The first page of "Short stories handed down . . . " written by Albert E. Coryer.
DONNA A. HIGGINS

My father was born September 19, 1845, on the old homestead his father had bought from the US at $1.25 per acre. The land was located in [the] town of Prairie du Chien about four miles northeast of the city of Prairie du Chien and the winter when Joseph was three years of age, Julian his father filled bags with wheat and loaded . . . his sleigh drawn by oxen and started for Gay's mill, which was a two-day trip: one day to get there (Mr. Gay ground the wheat during the night), then one day to get back. An old friend, Joseph Drew, was living with Julian at the time, thereby Mrs. Coryer and son Joseph were left at his mercy during Julian's trip to Gay's Mill.[2]

The evening Julian left at about sunset Mr. Drew hurriedly came in saying, "You are to have visitors for the night, Mrs. Coryer. There are many Indians coming over the hill coming this way." On looking Mrs. Coryer noticed many [Ho-Chunk] Indians coming.

Mrs. [Coryer] feared them. So she told Mr. Drew to be good to them and refuse them nothing they needed, to let them camp there if they desired; and it so happened Julian had plenty of hay which they wanted for their ponies and also to put on the ground to lay on in their teepees. The chief asked Mrs. Coryer if the [women who] had small papooses could get in the hut with her for the night; Mrs. welcomed them in.

It was very good that Mr. Drew understood and could speak the Indian language. There were several mothers with babies which crowded the hut very much. The babies were not accustomed to the warm indoor temperature and on being indoors for a while they all started to cry. The mothers took them outside about naked and tossed them about in the cold air. This caused the babies to go to sleep by laying them on deer hides that were stretched on the floor.

Mrs. Coryer managed to get food for the mothers in the house. Those outside in teepees cooked their own food. The Indians were fond of potatoes and it so happened that Julian had harvested and stored away in his cellar many bushels of potatoes. The Indians asked Mr. Drew for potatoes, which he did not refuse them, and for every one-half bushel of potatoes, they gave Mr. Drew a quarter of a venison which Mrs. had them pile in a corner of the log hut. By the time the Indians had enough potatoes, Mrs. had several quarters of venison.

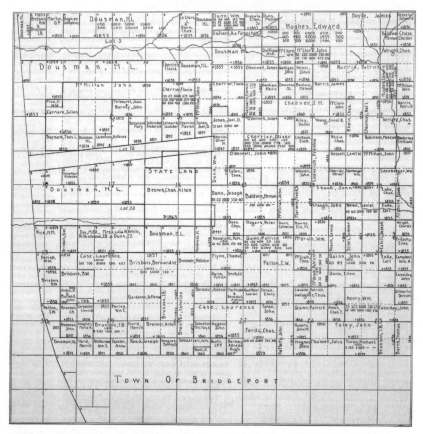

This plat map shows the two tracts of land acquired by Julian Carriere, located on the prairie and the bluffs north of Limery Coulee. *THE WISCONSIN DOMESDAY BOOK TOWN STUDIES*, VOL. 1, WISCONSIN HISTORICAL SOCIETY ARCHIVES

The night passed; morning came. The Indians were once more satisfied with food and then they packed up to leave on their way south; but before leaving each mother that had slept in the hut gave Joseph a string of beads, which loaded his neck to a breaking point, and also thanked Mrs. very much for welcoming them as she did.

Julian had venison to give to most of his friends, that which the Indians had left in exchange for potatoes. When he got home he found all this venison that had been stored away in the kitchen, which the Indians had brought in, and of course there was so much of it that they could never use it. So he loaded it in his sleigh box and took it around to his neighbors and relatives and gave it away so that it wouldn't go to waste.[3]

Living on the Land

When Julian first located here on his homestead there were no ditches washed out by rain. All ravines and coulees were round at the bottom and covered by a growth of native grass and brush and a spongy formation of grass and leaves, which would absorb the heavy rainfall and soak in the soft earth causing the springs to flow freely the year round. There were ponds of water here and there where the surface was such it held the water there.

Now the Mississippi River would overflow most of the valley quite often. When the settlers first settled here, a Mr. St. Jacque,* which came here from Canada and was a carpenter, would take contracts to build log houses. He went up the Wisconsin River to where there was pine trees growing near the river which were straight, and he would get enough of those logs for building, then rafted them down the Wisconsin River to the Mississippi River. Then he would pole them up the low gully west of Campion up as far as where the ballpark is now [in about 1950].** The river water extended there and was deep enough to raft the logs there. From there they were drawn by oxen to where they were used for building.[4]

Now when Julian Coryer first came to Prairie du Chien in 1829 the fur company he worked for would sometimes take a trip up the Mississippi River. When the water was high they would row their barges up along the bluffs from the mouth of the Mississippi River to the north end of the valley. Since then, the wash from the hills has filled in several feet. At that time the sandy soil reached to the foot of the hills; now there are several feet of black clay there which was washed down from the bluffs.

At that time the summers were short and cool, especially nights. Dent corn would not ripen: the only corn that would ripen was flint or Yankee corn, but other grain grew in abundance. Forty bushels of wheat was the average crop. Oats averaged eighty bushels per acre; now such grain averages about one half this number of bushels. This is due to hotter weather earlier in the season and on the reverse, most any dent corn does well and matures here.[5] Apples grew perfect without spraying: there were no insects then to cause apples or other fruit to be wormy. Winters were long

---

* A distant cousin of Albert's identified this person as Toussaint St. Jacques (1818–1896) born in Eastern Canada.
** The ballpark is Cecil Smith Field located in the 700 block of South Michigan Street.

and very cold. When Julian first settled here, winters were more severe. The snow fall averaged three feet every winter; the first big snowfall came before Christmas and stayed until sometime the first part of March when it started to melt. It kept it up and soon was all gone and then they had real springtime. Rain was very plentiful; this kept the springs and creek running strong all the time.[6] Wild fruit was plentiful: berries of different kinds—also plums very good and large—and a wild crab grew here. They were small and green and sour jelly could be made of them.

Game was plentiful: the wild pigeons were here by the millions. At times the flocks were so dense and large it caused a shadow as a large cloud does. The partridge, the prairie chicken, the quail, the duck, and geese brant, and many other waterfowl were plentiful.* Wild animals such as bear, wolf, fox, lynx, panther, wild cat, coon, mink, muskrat, beaver, otter, also the skunk. Man's friend the dog was very helpful those days protecting domestic animals from the wolf, the panther, wild cat, the lynx, also the dangerous reptile, the rattlesnake. Many human lives were saved by dogs those days. There were also many wolves here. The timber wolf grew to be about the size of a large collie dog or larger and about the color of the German police dog. They were vicious and killed young pigs and calves and . . . would tackle humans also. Until the state paid a bounty for killing them, then men went hunting them and killed them off.[7]

The settlers killed many wolves with snares made by bending down hickory saplings and tying the snare string at the top, fixed with bait of meat so that when the wolf pulled on the bait it let the sapling spring up so it would hang the wolf. Occasionally a dog was found hanging; this put this wolf killing out of commission.

In the 1840s or '50s timber did not grow dense as it grew later. The only trees then existing were large trees scattered here and there; on account of the dense growth of grass and fires from the grass, saplings could not get a start. But after the settlers stopped running fires by fighting them, the saplings got a start and grew so dense it killed off the growth of the wild or native grass which if the fires did run they were not so destructive. This second growth of timber got a start because the only fence material used by the settlers was rails of wood made by cutting the large oaks in logs

---

* Brant is a term commonly applied by some hunters to several varieties of geese.

about twelve feet, then splitting them in rails about three by four inches. It required much very strenuous labor. All that was fenced was the land that was under cultivation.[8]

Cattle, horses, and hogs had free range up to about the years of 1890 when the barb wire came in existence; then landowners started fencing in their pastureland.[9] At one time cutting and hauling hoop poles was quite an occupation. In winter they were bought at Wauzeka by meat packers to make hoops for pork barrels. They were cheaper and better than metal hoops on account of the salty brine that was used to preserve the pork.

Those hickory saplings grew so thick and dense. By cutting the sapling nine feet long, the top end was nearly as large as it was at the butt end, and without a knot or small limb they were tied in bundles of ten. They were about two inches in diameter; two hoops [were] made from each pole. This also took place in about 1880.

Joseph Coryer, my father, told me that on some of the hilltops before they broke up the virgin soil there were signs of cultivation [by Indians] before the white man came here. There were still the rows of where corn had been hilled up; the hills were in checks about three feet apart. The settlers first took up land near rivers because waterways were the only way of transportation before the railroads were built.

And sometimes the dealers were sold out of sugar. The settlers, to be sure of having sugar, they would get together and arrange it so a few of the men and boys stayed about the neighborhood whilst the others rigged up to go and make maple sugar on the Kickapoo River bottoms; the hard maple grew there in abundance.[10] The maple trees there were large and tall and would shed much sap which was very sweet. This sap was caught in small troughs made of wood during the winter. It was gathered about the grove in a barrel on [a] sleigh. It was boiled and evaporated in large iron kettles. It was boiled until it was thick enough that when poured in pans it would cool and become a hard cake of sugar.[11] The month of March is the month the maple gives out the sweet sap [from] which sugar is made. When they had made enough for all those included they broke camp and came home.

The settlers did not have the ways of canning fruit and meat as they now have. They had no glass jars or tin cans then: all they had was crock jars made of clay. The covers were sealed by melting bee's wax and pouring it over the top of the jar top. They dried most of the fruit. Plums were dried, also berries of different kind, also apples, and meat was salted and smoked to keep during the summer heat. People living in the country ate very little fresh meat during warm months of the year. The only place or way they had of keeping things cool was in a cellar or in a spring where cold water continually flowed or down in the well. It was difficult to get cream to [rise] on milk during summer: the milk would sour before the cream was raised. Cream separators were unknown up to about the year 1900.

Grocers bought dairy butter but paid no cash: the farmer had to trade it out. Eggs sold for as little as eight cents per dozen and also had to take trade groceries for their pay. Potatoes were sold by farmers for fifteen cents per bushel and had to buy groceries for the amount. Wheat was the only thing that brought cash and that sold as cheap as thirty-five cents per bushel. When farmers got to raising horses, good horses fit for cities brought good money: from one hundred up to two hundred dollars per head.

My grandfather, Thaddeus Langford, came from Chicago on his homestead three miles east of Eastman on Shanghai Ridge in the year 1854. The first year he was here, he accomplished little and as the riverboats burned wood for fuel to make steam, they wanted men to cut wood near Wauzeka. So Thaddeus and his brother-in-law Henry Bailey went there and cut wood during winter months, and they did not have time to raise pork. They had to buy it and [vendors] sold it at Wauzeka. So they bought a hog which dressed about two hundred pounds. They split the hog in halves and Saturday evening they left Wauzeka with each their one hundred pounds of pork on their shoulder. They left quite late in the evening and it soon got dark on the trail through the timber and the wolves scented the pork. They started to howl coming toward them. They were coming nearer so Bailey got frightened and said, "Now Thad, we had better drop this pork and run for our lives before the wolves get us." In answer Thaddeus said, "You can do as you please but I am not giving this hard-earned pork to the wolves. I will cut me a hickory club and I'll kill those wolves as they come."

Bailey could not stand it, so he dropped his pork and ran, but Thaddeus reached home with his pork. The wolves had their fill of Bailey's pork. The wives lived together whilst the men were gone and Bailey reached the place all frightened and told the women that no doubt Thaddeus "had been devoured by the wolves." Eliza walked the floor in fear of what was told her when suddenly she heard the sound of footsteps at the door. On opening it, Thaddeus entered, laid his pork on the table and said, "Let's have some of the pork to eat. I know Henry must be hungry after running as he did."

Another Adventure

Julian Coryer and Frank Gokey were married to sisters: Julian to Lucretia and Gokey to Mary Ann Lessard. Therefore [they] settled on land as that their land would join and be close neighbors when they first settled here in the early 1840s or earlier. They merely squatted on this land; they did not have the cash to pay Uncle Sam; thereby they intended to make the money by raising wheat. The sowing, harvesting, and threshing all had to be done by manual labor. The sowing was done by the sower having a bag of wheat in a bag fastened over his shoulder and the grain scattered by hand. The land was plowed with oxen. Many made their plows of wood and after sowing, it was buried in ground by harrows, also made of wood. They were made this shape, also drawn by oxen, and the wild pigeons were so many that it was difficult for the sower to get the grain covered before the pigeon would pick it up to eat.

Then the cutting of the grain, when ripe, was done with what was named the cradle. This tool was made up of a broad scythe and curved sticks compared in shape and length to the scythe. There were four of the curved sticks. The handle had a queer curve to it so that when swinging it the user could lay the grain in rows so it could be gathered in bundles with a rake and so that the heads of grain were all at one end of the bundle. A band to tie this bundle was made with some of the longest straws. The cradle was made this fashion. The rake entirely of wood was about sixteen inches wide with a long handle about six feet. This [was] the tool for harvesting. Now the flail . . . used to thresh out the grain was made of two round sticks, one about three feet long and about two inches in diameter, the other about five feet long and one and a half inches in diameter. The short stick was the part that did the striking; the longer was the handle part. The sticks were fastened together by a strong and durable leather string well-oiled and fastened to the short stick so that it could be used by merely whirling

Coryer's drawings of the cradle tool used for harvesting grain. WISCONSIN HISTORICAL SOCIETY ARCHIVES

the long stick this fashion. When the grain had been shelled, the straw was taken away with a fork. Many farmers did not even have a metal fork; they made a fork of a limb that had three prongs. Then the grain was cleaned or separated from chaff by taking it in a shovel or other container and pouring it so as to let the wind blow away the chaff from the grain. You can now realize the labor and time it took to get wheat ready to sell.

As I mentioned in the start of this story, the settlers had little money; therefore they merely squatted on a forty [acre tract] of land, building log buildings the best they could with little tools. They did not have lumber; therefore they had no lumber floors. The clay was smoothed and packed hard and that was the floor. The roof was made of rafters made from straight saplings about four inches in diameter, then other saplings split and fastened horizontally across to the rafters about one foot apart; they had no nails, thereby they used wooden pegs instead.

Then the shingles were made by sawing large oaks in blocks about eighteen inches long, then the shingles were made by splitting the blocks with a tool made of steel made comparatively to a knife blade but about eighteen inches long. They split those shingles about one-quarter-inch thick. A wooden mallet was used to strike the large knife. Those shingles were fastened to the horizontal-laid sticks on the roof.

The only lumber they had was made by splitting logs in thin strips, then hewing those strips down to boards or planks. Windows were few because glass was scarce and expensive. A fireplace was their only way they had for heating and doing their cooking. Those fireplaces were made of rock and clay was used to fill in between rocks. The place where the fire was built was about four or five feet wide. The chimney gradually was built to about two feet at the top. A long-handled frying pan was used for frying things over the fire. A long crane-like iron fastened to the side of [the] fireplace was made so as to swing and hold a kettle for boiling purposes. The baking was done by making a large oven with rocks and clay mortar the size about five feet long and three feet square. They built a hot fire in this oven so as to get the rocks hot, then the fire was scraped out and the bread or cake in pans were shoved in this hot oven and a door was closed tight to hold the heat to a baking temperature and kept there until baked.

They got their water either from springs or they dug wells and curbed them with rock. Those wells were dug down to the water level or deeper and water was drawn up by using a wooden bucket and a rope or chain. The well was about three feet in diameter.

This gives you an idea of what the settler had to do before he could start making money to pay for his land and as [yet] Julian Coryer and Frank Gokey had not got around to make money to pay for their forty-acre claim.

HERCULES DOUSMAN VISITS

And this was on a cold winter day Julian had hewn parts for to assemble into a sleigh and he had brought the parts in the log hut to assemble. His son Joseph, then a small boy, was watching his father work. Joseph suddenly said, "Somebody is coming." As Julian looked out, he saw Mr. Dousman in his cutter.[12] A cutter was a light sleigh drawn by a horse. Mr. Dousman tied his horse and blanketed it and took in his large robe made of buffalo hide. This robe had been presented to Mr. Dousman by the Indians he dealt with; the Indians had decorated this robe with beads assembled so as to form a beautiful decoration, and [as] Mr. Dousman entered the hut, he laid the robe over a chair; thereby Joseph amused himself by looking at the beautiful robe.

Julian greeted Mr. Dousman and asked him to let him put his horse in the log stable and also to take his heavy fur overcoat. Mr. Dousman answered by saying he could not stay long, that he had come to deliver a message. And said, "I came up to tell you that I have had the forty acres you have settled on, and also the forty acres Gokey is on, entered and that you will have to find yourself another forty-acre tract to live on." This angered Julian because he had always considered Dousman as a friend; thereby Julian said, "Now Dousman, I considered you a friend and if you did me and Gokey such a deal it makes me feel like not letting you go looking as fresh as you are now."

Dousman now knew he [had] gone far enough, so he said, "Julian, it does me good to realize you still have the old fighting spirit you had when we worked for the fur company. Now I did not come to take your land away from you; but I have come to help you from losing it." Mr. Dousman said, "As I was in the local land office this morning I overheard a conversation between two strangers that are planning on going to Mineral Point to the US land office and have your forty acres and also Gokey's forty acres entered, then they can order you off."

Julian then apologized for having shown his anger and thanked Dousman for having been so kind. Mr. Dousman then said, "This is only a friendly act. Now you and Gokey must get to Mineral Point before tomorrow morning to get ahead of those strangers."

Julian said, "But neither myself or Gokey have the money and only one horse to get there with." Mr. Dousman then said, "I realized that, so I will loan you and Gokey the money and you and Gokey get in my cutter with me and lead your horse back of the cutter to my place and I will let you have my harness and cutter. And I also have the description of your land ready so all you do is get there as soon as possible and on getting there tomorrow do not lose time. Tie and blanket your horse and get in the land office at once before the others get there and get your land away from you."

Julian hurried and got Gokey and his horse and they hurried to get Mr. Dousman home. Then they started on their way to Mineral Point. It was very cold and the snow was deep; thereby it made it hard for the horse to draw the cutter. Night overtook them. It was difficult to hold their bearing so as not to get lost and wolves were plentiful.... [The wolves] got so bold they wanted to tackle them or the horse. They cut a hickory pole and one drove the horse whilst the other beat off the wolves with the pole. But they made it, they got in Mineral Point just before the clerk came to the office; but they waited at the door and entered and laid the description of their land and money Mr. Dousman had helped them with and just as the clerk had made out their deeds, the two strangers Mr. Dousman had told them of entered and on presenting their papers the clerk answered saying, "You are too late. Those two men just have had those two forty [acre tracts] entered." Thereby Mr. Dousman did them a very good and friendly act which Coryer and Gokey never forgot.

HERCULES DOUSMAN

Coryer provided more details on Hercules Dousman in his interview with Florence Bittner:

MRS. BITTNER: Are there any other stories of Mr. Dousman that perhaps would be interesting?

MR. CORYER: Yes, I must say that Mr. Dousman was very kind and willing to help the old settlers and also very forgiving if ever the settlers would trespass on his land or do anything that wasn't just as it should be about his property.

Now for one thing, he owned the Mill Coulee and also owned the creek which runs down this coulee, and there was much trout in this creek. And the settlers' boys would go down there occasionally during the summer and catch trout, and Mr. Dousman realized that they were apt to do that, so he'd sneak up on them, catch the boys doing this, and he'd say, "Now, boys, I've caught you taking my trout. Now you'll have to give me that trout which you've caught (which no doubt they had several of them)—now you go home and leave my trout alone. This is my creek and my trout."

"Yes, Mr. Dousman, we're sorry. Yes, we'll do that, Mr. Dousman." And the boys would leave and go on towards home for a short distance, then stop and watch Mr. Dousman disappear, go back and catch whatever trout they needed for themselves and go home and have their trout. And that happened many a time.

And then another thing was, the lines of the different sections of land wasn't very well established and the old settlers sometimes would

continued on next page

overreach and go over on Dousman's and chop wood and cord wood, four feet long, of course, which they sold to the boats. The boats at the time used wood for fueling their boilers and these old settlers sold their wood there. Well, Mr. Dousman would catch them cutting wood on his land and he'd go to them and he'd say, "Well, I see you've been cutting wood on my land."

"Well, yes, I've cut wood there, but that's on my land, isn't it, Mr. Dousman? That can't be on your land."

"Oh, no, you're on my land."

"Well, I'm sorry. I didn't realize I was cutting on your land, Mr. Dousman."

"Well, I'll have that," Mr. Dousman would say, "I'll have that wood hauled home. I need fuel too. And you'll have to cut some more and cut it on your own land."

"Well, now, Mr. Dousman, I have to have that money. I have to have it soon, too, because it's about time that I should haul it, before the roads break up and the sleighing plays out. I've got to have that money for taxes and other things that I need, for buying clothing for my children, and also other things about the house. I'm sorry. I can't very well spare that wood. Can't you let me have it?"

"Well, yes, you take the wood this time. Don't you cut any more now. You sure don't cut anymore wood on my land."

"All right, Mr. Dousman, I'll do that. I'll be careful." And in a short time the thing was repeated again and again but Mr. Dousman was always willing to forgive and never punish....

Now, this land that Mr. Dousman owned was previously owned by Mr. Rolette, and Mr. Dousman had been Mr. [Joseph] Rolette's secretary for several years, and after Mr. Rolette's death, Mr. Dousman married his widow [Jane Fisher], and then, of course, then this land, the title had been turned over to Dousman. This was considered the Dousman estate. And before this, Mr. Rolette getting this land and it was first entered by, from the government, by a man the name of [Henry] Fisher. And Mr. Rolette married Mr. Fisher's daughter and thereby he became the owner some way of this Mill Coulee land, and ... the creek still bears the name of Fisher

continued on next page

Creek. It's on record on all game law records as Fisher Creek. And this creek was also used . . . for running a flour mill. Mr. William Mosier built the flour mill about a quarter of a mile from the mouth of the coulee, and then built a dam up the coulee about another quarter of a mile, and then the mill race from the dam to the mill, and used this water, this power, for running his mill. And he made good flour, and it was a good mill for the times. And it still it wasn't a paying proposition. There wasn't enough . . . settlers around to make it a paying proposition, and finally Mr. Mosier built a mill over at Marquette, Iowa, and this mill in Marquette, Iowa, was a much more paying proposition.[13] And also, when it comes back to Mr. Dousman owning the lands, later on, the Dousmans . . . bought the Campbell Coulee . . . which was a very good tract of land. Thereby the Dousmans owned much of the land about Prairie du Chien.

JULIAN GETS LAND GRANT OF 160 ACRES

From Coryer's manuscript "The Life of Julian Coryer"
A few years after Julian had settled to farming at Prairie du Chien he received notice that he was entitled to 160 acres of land located in Nebraska about where Omaha now is. At the time it was a wilderness. The Indians were quite hostile and the US government planned this to get it settled by giving each Black Hawk veteran 160 acres. This would cover quite a territory with men which were accustomed to the Indian and could defeat the Indian if necessary.

Julian was accustomed to this wild life and at the same time knew this would develop to be a good farming district because he had noticed the wonderful growth of wild vegetation that grew there. He had noticed this as he traveled the Missouri River whilst employed in the . . . fur company service. But when he mentioned this to his wife she refused to go. And when Judge Brunson learned of this, he offered Julian enough money for the 160 acres in Nebraska so Julian could buy 160 acres of government

continued on next page

land adjoining the forty acres he had previously bought, making Julian a 200-acre tract of land.

Judge Brunson was [a] government surveyor and also knew the land allotted [allocated to] Julian and realized that it would be valuable as soon as the country became settled by the whites. Julian sold it because he would [have] lost it if he did not settle on it within a certain time after it had been [allocated] to him.

When the settler first started farming he sowed no grass; see, he depended on the wild grasses for hay to feed his horses and cattle. Before the Picardee Coulee was plowed up for raising crops, this coulee was noted for its producing good wild grasses for hay.* Therefore anyone that wanted hay would go and cut hay there. So Julian and his son Joseph, which was then about twelve years of age, went to this coulee with [scythes] to cut hay. They had cut only a few strokes when they had to kill a rattler to proceed. They kept finding them and by the time they had cut a square of fifty feet, they had killed seven rattlers. This disheartened Julian so he said to Joseph, "Let's hitch up our horses and get out of here," leaving the hay they had cut. No doubt the snakes were in there feeding on frogs which lived in the grass.

---

* Picatee Coulee is the present name.

PASSENGER PIGEONS AND PANTHERS

By the time Joseph was twelve years of age, Julian had three good yoke of oxen and had all the land he wanted to till broken and he broke or ploughed land for others. This breaking plow was built very strong: the beam at the heaviest was six inches thick and a foot wide. This plow would turn a furrow two feet wide and would plow under hickory saplings three inches at the stump.

It was quite a job after this land was plowed. Those saplings and hazel brush had to be shaken out and piled up and burned before the land could be harrowed ready to plant or sow to crops. Three yoke of oxen [were] used to pull this plow. Joseph drove three yoke of oxen at the age of twelve years whilst his father held the plow.

The wild pigeon[s] were so thick and bold that it was hard for the farmer to sow his grain and get it harrowed in before the pigeon[s] picked it up because they were thousands of them come in a flock. So Julian would put in a light load of powder in the gun and have Joseph stand by with the gun as he sowed his grain. Joseph was a small boy, but he could shoot the gun when the pigeons were about to light to eat the wheat, thereby . . . frightening them away and giving Julian time to harrow in the grain. The pigeon[s] [were] also destructive to the grain in the fall, when the grain ripened. In the fall, when the wheat got ripe, the pigeons would come from the north again, and they'd just about destroy the crops before they could get it harvested and put in stacks in barns.[14]

As the farmers complained much that the pigeon[s] [were] a nuisance and destructive, the pastors of all the Catholic churches along the Mississippi Valley arranged it by getting permission of their bishop to make a novena. This novena was made to exile the pigeon for ninety-nine years.

This novena was made in the early 1860s, and it worked because it was not long before the pigeon was extinct. They flew east and apparently tried to cross the Atlantic Ocean because millions dropped in with [the] tide so that they laid in windrows along the shore. Farmers hauled them on their land for fertilizer. There were a few that lingered about for a few years. I, the writer born in 1877, and was then about [nine years] of age, saw two, a pair of them. My father shot them, thereby I tasted of the last pigeons. Thereby the pigeon should be back with us in the early 1960s.

About the year 1930 the wildlife commission offered $2,500 for a pair of the wild pigeon[s], but apparently there was not a pair in existence. Now, did you ever meditate on the total nonexistence of wild birds? The wild pigeon is the only wild bird that disappeared in so short a time and so early. Several other kinds of bird have disappeared to a few just of late but a few can be found somewhere. Thereby it proves that the pigeon was not killed off by man and that the novena was the cause of their disappearing in so short a time.

When the first white men came here the pigeons were here by the millions.[15] The main food of the wild pigeon[s] was acorns and beechnuts and

CORYER'S OPTIMISM ON PASSENGER PIGEONS

Passenger pigeons, once plentiful in North America, died out in the early twentieth century due to overhunting and habitat decline. Albert Coryer, however, believed that prayer exiled the pigeons and that they would return. Interviewed for an article appearing in the *Capital Times* (Madison) on September 19, 1960, "Coryer, 83, Adds a Footnote to History," Albert said he believed that the pigeons would return in 1962. If they did, he said, "In 1962, it will be different simply because if the birds do come—in great numbers—there will be many more farmers in the Prairie du Chien area to scare them away than there were in those far off years." Coryer expanded on this belief in his interview with historian Florence Bittner:

> So they began to complain very much about the pigeons; and the pastors of the churches . . . all through the valley and the eastern part of the United States got together and talked the thing over and decided that they could make a novena and drive those pigeons out of the country. They thought it would be right as long as the settlers wanted it that way, and which they did. They made a novena, the novena of the nine-day prayer, or nine-day way of devotion by, with prayer, and hearing Mass every morning. And the settlers were so devout and were so bound to get the pigeons driven away from here; this was in the last part of March in about 1862 that this happened, during the 1860s, and the farmers got so that they couldn't travel with horses or oxen anymore, the roads got so muddy. They'd walk, even walk ten miles every morning, and they finally made the novena as they should, and in about two years there [were] hardly any pigeons left. The first year even, they of course were exiled, what they call exiling them, meaning they were to go out to some other country across the waters. And the pigeons all went to the Atlantic Ocean and tried to fly across the ocean, and many of them fell in. And the tide would bring them in on shore in real windrows [banks or ridges created by wind] and the farmers along the East Coast would haul them on their land and plow them under for fertilizer. And that

continued on next page

was the way most of them went away. There were a few scattering flocks that remained for several years afterwards, but they were very few and didn't do any damage. That's the way the pigeons were sent away, and they are supposed to return in ninety-nine years. They were exiled for ninety-nine years and then they're supposed to return in ninety-nine years, from 1862, you see.

seed from native grasses and weeds. Often they emigrated from the south in the spring of the year. It seemed they flew up much in great flocks. People that lived here at Prairie du Chien said the flocks were large enough they covered the entire valley and so dense that it caused a shadow the same as a dense large cloud would. But later there were flocks of thousands that would fly south in the evening and back up north in the morning. The flocks would travel over the edge of the bluffs and would fly merely high enough to miss the tree tops and hazel. The flocks were long, long but not wide.

And then they would go over the hilltops. They wouldn't fly from one hilltop to [the] other but swoop down into the coulee and then up on the other side, just barely missing the tops of the trees and hazel brush. When the settlers first came here, those hills weren't covered with this second-growth timber. There [were] large trees here and there, and then in between those trees, there was much hazel brush and also this prairie hay, a very nutritious kind of hay that grew there. And those pigeons would just barely miss all this.[16]

Mrs. Coryer never bothered the men by asking them to get her pigeon[s] for cooking; she had a long slender pole, and she would get where those flocks [came] over by standing in the hazel brush. The pigeon[s] would fly all about her. She would soon have all the pigeon[s] she wanted by striking at the flock with her pole. Some would catch them with nets; they would skin the pigeon and merely save the breast and legs and pickled them for winter use.

The settlers would also salt them down, or pickle them down for winter. They'd make nets out of strings, compared to a fish net, and fasten them to a frame, and then they'd pick out a clean spot, scatter grain there, and put this net, set this net there with a stick under one end and it wouldn't be long; but the pigeons would know where this grain was, and they'd come there by the thousands. And they'd have a string, of course, from this stick out to where they could hide somewhere, out back of hazel brush, or something like that and when the net was filled with pigeons they'd just pull the stick and they'd have dozens of pigeons under this net. And they'd go around and break the necks of the pigeons. They wouldn't stop and pick them, picking the feathers off, they'd just merely skin them and keep the meaty parts, the breasts and legs of the pigeons, salt 'em down for winter, so they had pigeons for the winter.[17]

Were there panthers here? Yes, my father had a young man working for him on the farm. This man on a Sunday went to town and on his return late in evening and very dark and as he was about to ascend the hill to the house he heard something back of him. On looking he noticed the two fiery eyes of an animal; on taking close notice he realized by the size, length, and all appearance it was a panther. It kept gaining on him so he decided he would take off his coat so he could get along faster and the animal got very close and was snarling, therefore the man threw the coat at the animal. The animal pounced on the coat and devoured it to shreds. This gave the man a chance to run up the hill, but the animal was soon near him again, so he tossed his vest at it. This stopped him for a while whilst he riddled the vest, then the animal got near him again so the man flung his hat at the animal. By this time he had drawn the dogs' attention: by his calling, the dogs came in time to save him by chasing the panther away.

ANOTHER STORY CONCERNING THE PANTHERS

Joseph Coryer had a large sow which had ten pigs and when the pigs grew to about twenty pounds each they disappeared one at a time, about one to every two days. Joseph could not determine what was taking the pigs because the sow was strong and ugly. After six of the pigs had disappeared, Joseph just made up his mind of finding out what happened to his pigs, so he kept watch from evening on through the night with a gun ready and his dogs on the watch. The second night it was very dark. Suddenly he heard a pig squeal, and then the sow got excited and he saw a large animal leap out of the pen. It was so dark he did not shoot, but the dogs gave the animal a chase and the panther went up a tree. Joseph and his brother-in-law Orville Langford made a torch of birch bark by fastening the bark to the end of a long pole so they could see it and shoot it, but when the torch was raised the animal leaped [a great] distance away. They could not shoot it, and the dogs could not overtake the panther. It made its getaway but did not come back for more pigs.

Now to the Bear

Joseph Coryer was born in 1845. . . . In the fall of the year and [when] hickory nuts were ripe, Joseph was then a boy of ten years and with his cousins they went picking nuts. Of course the dogs followed, and as the boys were picking nuts the dogs tracked a bear and overtook it. The bear tried to drive the dogs away, but he soon decided to climb a tree and the boys' attention was taken up by the turmoil. They ran to see what was up. They soon noticed the bear in the tree, so the boys all ran home to tell their father[s] of it. The fathers came back with them, bringing their rifle, and shot the bear.

When the settlers first came here the deer was plentiful. Up to the year 1870 they were many, sometimes herds of them as many as twenty in a herd. Then came the bad winter: in December about one foot of snow fell and finished with rain, which caused a crust of ice. Then about the first of January another fall of one foot of snow with a crust of ice of one-quarter inch of ice. Then the deer died by the thousand. The crust of ice was strong enough to hold the deer up if it walked. But as soon as it leaped, when it come down it would break through those crusts of ice, and by struggling to get out they would cut their legs up so they bled much and got weak and sore and some broke their legs. The only feed they had was the white oak leaves they could reach on the trees. Some wintered by living about the farmers' haystacks. The old settlers made money by skinning the dead deer. They were paid one dollar per hide. Some would skin and bring in ten hides a day. One man worked so hard at it he got pneumonia and died. What few deer lived through this winter were killed off by hunters in a few years. The deer were extinct in the southeastern part of the state of Wisconsin up to the year 1930 or about then. The state brought in a few to the state park and they were protected by the game laws so the deer bred up to where they are now in 1950 to be quite plentiful and can be killed during the permitted season.

The quail was nearly extinct after this hard winter. The only quail that wintered were those quail that lived about the straw stacks.... They would huddle next to a log or brush pile to get shelter and the snow drifted over them and smothered or starved them. As Joseph Coryer was in the woods to get a load of wood, he had to go ahead of his team of horses and break the crusts of ice because the horses would cripple themselves trying to break their way through the deep snow and ice. As he was going along slashing his way through with his axe, he heard the sound of quails under the snow. He went to where the sound came and soon was where he could trace the spot where the birds were. On using his axe he soon realized the birds were huddled near a log, so he went home, built a cage, and drove the birds in the cage. Twelve of them he kept in the attic, and they all lived until springtime. Then Joseph let them go at liberty. This helped replenish the quail, but they were scarce from then on. Before this happened, quail were plentiful. The prairie chicken was also very plentiful up to this winter; but from then on they were not so plentiful so that which were left were killed off by hunters. This all took place in Crawford County and there about.

FARM ANIMALS

You may think why the old settlers used oxen instead of horses. There were different reasons. One reason was that the horses they then had were small and light and very lively, thereby were not well fit for heavy pulling such as breaking land or hauling heavy loads. The oxen were heavier, shorter legged, and more powerful and lazy, did not get excited and could stand hard work with less grain. Plenty of hay or grass would hold them up.

Another reason was that all the oxen needed to work with [were] a yoke and chain and a ring fastened to [the] yoke. The yoke was made of wood; thereby they cost nothing, merely the labor in making it. The chain was to pull with the ring for holding up the end of wagon or sleigh tongue. To control [the] oxen all [that] was used was a whip. The whip had to be quite long, made of a small pole and a lash made of leather. The stick or pole was about eight feet long so that when the driver wanted the oxen to stop or back up they could hit the oxen on the nose with the whip. The oxen soon learned the command of the driver and there was very little use of the whip. The word "gee" meant to turn to the right. The word "haw" meant to turn to the left. "Whoa" meant stop. "Get up" meant to start or go faster.

Now to workhorses, one had to have a harness which should be made by a harness maker and cost money which the old settlers did not have much of. It took the best of leather for making harnesses, many buckles, snaps, and rings. The horse was harder to train to work, especially those broncos which was then used. Later the heavy draft type of horses were imported from Europe. They were better for heavy work; they had the weight and were not so easily excited. The early horses were best for traveling fast and long distances.

Nearly every farmer raised a few sheep for wool because each housewife would spin yarn, then knit mittens, socks, and stockings for the family. The home knit goods were more durable and warmer than those woven by machines.

Now before the Milwaukee Railroad came to Prairie du Chien, the only sale for hogs was in the early winter [to] the wealthy men that employed many men in the north woods, which was then near St. Paul, Minnesota, and Chippewa Falls, Wisconsin. Those men had the best of the pine timber and hauled it to the riverbank with oxen and horses. When the ice went out of the river those logs were formed in rafts and were taken down to sawmills along the river. At one time there was a very large sawmill at Prairie du Chien. This mill sawed all sorts of lumber shingles and laths. In about 1890 this mill was moved to St. Louis, Missouri.

Now back to selling pork, those men which had this timber cut had large camps where many men were fed so they could stand this strenuous work and exposure to cold. The employers would come down to Prairie du Chien in December as soon as the ice on the Mississippi River would be thick enough to carry loads and horses or oxen to draw them on sleighs. Those men would buy all the dressed hogs they could get and beef also, but beef was not plentiful. They paid only two to three cents a pound for dressed hogs.

There was very little beef raised because it seems that the settlers didn't care to raise cattle. They weren't prepared to house them in the winter. They had no barns and they didn't have the ways of housing them and so they didn't raise many cattle. They just kept a few cows, and what male animals were kept over were used as oxen, so there wasn't much beef raised, but very much pork because they used to sell this pork to . . . the lumbermen that came down from the north. The old-timers used to call them the "silk-hats." They all wore those high silk hats and a silk, black silk handkerchief around their neck, and long black coats dressed, of course, as the wealthy men did in the cities at that time. And the old-timers called them "silk-hats." "We'll have to get our hogs ready." That was late in the fall or early in the winter they'd start . . . getting their hogs ready for butchering.[18]

The farmers got together and helped one another butcher and dress the hogs and when they had them all dressed and frozen, the lumbermen would hire all the farmers with teams of horses or oxen to haul this pork up to St. Paul, Minnesota, or thereabout to the lumber camps. The frozen hogs were loaded on wood racks. There were many teams go up at once and would travel single file and not too close to each other so as not to put too much weight in one spot. Some men went ahead of the teams and tried the ice with axes to be sure no one would break through the ice and very seldom anything happened to them.

And they'd go up the river, forty, about forty teams at once, loaded with pork. . . . Every ten minutes the head team would pull out and the next team would take the lead and the head team would drop in back so that would rest the teams, because, of course, there were no roads tracked—deep snow—and that's the way they got their meat up to the north woods for lumbering at the time.[19]

Now you wonder how the farmers could raise hogs and sell them at so small a price. Well, as I mentioned before, hogs had free range and got most of their feed in the woods. Acorns and nuts [were] what they ate most of the time. Wild artichokes also grew and the hogs would root them up and eat them, and the Mississippi River lowlands was a great place for hogs during the summer season. Hogs thrived on the roots, grass, weeds, and clams, claw fish [crawfish], etc., they found in sloughs and swamps. The farmers would take the sows and small pigs across certain sloughs on islands and they would stay there until early winter. When the ice got strong enough to carry them, the farmers got together and rounded the hogs up and drove them home.

Now each farmer had a certain mark on the sows they put in the islands. They marked them on the ear. One farmer's mark was a round hole in left ear; another's mark was a hole in right ear; another was a V cut out in left ear; the other was a V in right ear, and in fall when they rounded them up whatever pigs followed a sow those pigs belonged to the owner of the sow. Thereby sometimes a farmer put only one sow in the islands and twenty pigs followed her; it was considered that those pigs belonged to the owner of the sow bearing his mark. And [when] another put three sows in [the] islands and only twenty followed his three sows, he had to be satisfied with the twenty pigs.

There were unjust men at the time as there are unjust men now in taking advantage of others when opportunity permitted to cheat. Each hog owner that turned one or more than one brood sow in the islands or woods would mark her by cutting certain marks in the ear or ears. Now when the time came to round up the hogs in the fall or autumn, the young hogs or shoats were not marked, so the tricky ones would get there first and get as many young hogs to follow his sow or sows as possible. Some of them would boast of how well his sows did by averaging twenty pigs each sow, which was something impossible.[20]

When those hogs reached the farm, they were penned up and fed grain to fatten them and also to give the meat the grain flavor. Otherwise the meat would taste fishy after those hogs living in islands on clams and claw-fish [crawfish] and roots out of the water.

Now those hogs got vicious and would attack a person. If he would come on them suddenly and surprise them they would attack a lone person. My father went duck hunting in the fall of the year and as he was walking through the grass and weeds he suddenly [came] on a drove of hogs. There were several large old sows. They all started grunting and made for him. He had a gun, single barrel with shot, but he knew that if he shot and caused one to squeal, it would anger the hogs worse, so he ran for a tree and got up in it. Luckily he had a small dog with him and the dog kept barking and teasing the hogs until they got going at the dog. This gave him a chance to get down and run the opposite direction and get away. The breed of hogs they had then were not like the hogs farmers raised nowadays: they were rangy, long legged, and had a long nose, and their ears stood up. They called them razorbacks, but they could stand more grief and live on little feed.

WILL-O-THE-WISP

Those incidents written below happened before the year 1880. Now to the story of the will-o-the-wisp.[21] This is considered by most people to be something mysterious, but it is not. The "will-o-the-wisp" did exist and was quite natural. Some will say it did not exist elsewhere than on swampy or low lands and it was caused by gases or fumes from decayed wood or vegetation which would cause light which could be seen on dark nights; but my father and other old-timers told me that which proves to be logical.

This happened up on top of the bluffs. My grandfather had a young man living with him and this fellow was accustomed to going to the neighbors and spending evenings there with the young folk living there. One evening after the evening meal the young man intended to go to one of the near neighbors. [He] looked out the window the direction he intended to go. There was a road that led there. This road crossed the line between my grandfather's land and the neighbor adjoining him. There was a line fence there and a gate at the crossing of the road. There [was] a large tall post at each end of this gate. This gate could be seen by looking out the window which the young man was looking and kept looking for some time. My grandfather noticed him staring out this window so he asked him what he was staring at. The young fellow answered by saying there is two strange lights playing about the gate posts up on the hilltop. So Granddad went to the window and on looking he saw the lights, which would change in size from the size of a candlelight to the size of a peck measure, which would be about ten inches in diameter. The lights would gradually change either to large or small.

So Granddad said to the young fellow, "Let's go up there and see what those lights are." On getting near the lights, which were on the top of the large gate post, and as they got near, the lights moved some distance and set on other posts. As they moved (which was about as fast as a bird can fly), it left a thread-like stream of light as it moved comparative to the June lightening bug, only the stream of light was larger. When the light stopped on the post it moved to, it remained small for some time, then gradually would get larger. The men followed it, and when they would get about so close, it would move and set on a tree or fence. So they realized they had better not try to track it down for fear it would cause them to get lost. Then later my father and a neighbor went spearing fish. Those days they speared fish by night. They would peel birch bark. This bark would burn the same as if it had been soaked in oil. They would get a green stick of wood about five feet long and three inches in diameter, fasten it on the end of the boat, and put the birch bark at the other end of the stick and light it.

This would give a light so the men could see the fish in the water quite a distance. Indians would spear fish by day when the ice got thick enough to carry a man. They would cut a hole in the ice about one foot in diameter and lay grass or weeds on the ice, then lay on their stomach on the hay, then cover their head and the hole in the ice with a robe or blanket, holding the spear in one hand and when a fish crossed by the hole they could see it and spear it.

Now back to when my father and friend went spearing in Grimard Lake: and as they were going slowly along the water's edge they saw a light on a tree near the shore, and as they got near it, it moved from that tree to another tree down the line. So they put the oars in the oar rings and started to row, trying to find out what it was. As I explained before, it would leave a thread-like light behind itself when it moved from place to place and would give a candle-size light when it would first set, then the light would get larger; they gave up the chase for fear it would lead them too far.

Now a Mr. La Roque was out coon hunting in the Mississippi lowlands, and as he was going about to follow his dogs he [came] on to one of the "will-o-the-wisp" and followed it until he got near enough to reach it by gunshot. As the blaze got to a large size, he up and shot at it and the light suddenly went out on shooting it. So he went on hunting coons, but the next day he went where [the] light was which he shot at. On the ground under the tree laid a dead bird of a kind [neither] he, Mr. La Roque, nor anyone else had ever seen. Thereby this is evidence that the "will-o-the-wisp" was a rare bird which would give light by some action of its wings, comparatively to the fire bug which can be seen on a dark night in the month of June. The will-o-the-wisp was seldom seen, thereby the birds were few, and as Mr. La Roque shot one, others did the same, and the bird was exterminated. Now we see no more of the will-o-the-wisp.

Short Stories Concerning Indians

About the year 1850, the men in charge of civil authority discovered . . . a girl living with Indians here at Prairie du Chien (what tribe I do not know). This girl apparently of white ancestry and of which the Indians did not deny, but would not give up any information pertaining to her coming among of them. The authorities took her from the Indians. The girl then about ten years of age could speak no other language other than the Indian language. Thereby the authorities had to find her a home where someone could converse with her in the Indian language. Julian Coryer could speak the language so the men in charge . . . after taking her away from the Indians made arrangements with Julian and his wife to care of her.

The girl was not vicious, but was inclined to keep up the Indian ways of living. She did not care to learn to do things whites did, but finally with patience used by those caring for her she became and grew up as one of the white race. When [the] Coryers first took her in charge, she occasionally would wander out in the woods, apparently trying to meet some of the tribe. Julian taught her her catechism and prayers, preparing her for first communion; thereby she became a Catholic. After living a few years with [the] Coryers she went to work for Frank Lessards; from there she and a Miss Plaunt went to work in St. Paul, Minnesota. She was baptized Mary Kaween, because Kaween was what the Indians called her.[22]

This happened in the late 1850s. A band of Indians camped and lived not far from Coryer's home and occasionally would come for things [they] needed, and [the] Coryers were always there to do the best they could by them; and towards spring they came and asked to borrow a sleigh and harness. They had ponies and wanted it to take a sick old woman of their tribe to one of their doctors elsewhere. Coryer let them have an outfit thinking that would be the last of it; but to his surprise, in the beginning of the following winter, the Indians brought the sleigh back in good condition. And thanked [the] Coryers for the use of the sleigh.

The Indians had much respect for Mr. [Hercules] Dousman Sr. . . . The Indians would not go up to the Villa Louis door without being beckoned or called up by Mr. Dousman.[23]

Now when Mr. Dousman died, his wife sent word to Julian Coryer of his death. Mr. Dousman and Mr. Coryer met and got acquainted whilst they both worked for the fur company with headquarters in St. Louis, Missouri. Dousman was one of the company's secretaries, and Coryer helped the company in transferring different articles which the company had imported from England to trade to the Indians for furs. Those articles were transported to the company's forts in the far northwestern part of the US and Canada, where the most valuable furs could be obtained from the Indians. The articles Indians cared for the most were rifles and ammunition. The traders would get valuable furs worth thousands of dollars for a rifle and some ammunition. Alcohol was also in much demand by the Indians. The company had to be careful not to let them have much at a time, and they would dilute it with water so that the Indians would [not] get intoxicated and then they would get in trouble that might cause bloodshed.

Beads, thread, needles, calicoes, blankets, and many other articles—salt was a great money maker for the company. The company sold salt a dollar a pint to their workmen whilst they paid their workmen ten dollars a month for their labor and standing chances of being killed by the Indians. The company traveled by water up the Missouri River as far as they could by barges which were manned by ten men with one large oar each. On reaching the source of the river they transferred their cargo to a fort. Then those articles were loaded on ponies trained for that purpose, each pony carrying about twenty pounds each to faraway forts in the northwest, and dogs were also used for collecting the valuable furs in the far north. The men working at this lived mostly on dried buffalo meat. It needed no cooking and would go farther than any other food of its weight, and there was no waste. Furs were transferred to St. Louis the same route, only reverse direction to which the articles for trading were transferred.

Now back to Mr. Dousman's death: as I mentioned in the beginning of this story, Coryer was notified of Dousman's death. As they had been friends for many years, Coryer realized it was his duty to go to Dousmans' and show the relatives his sympathy toward them. As Coryer and his son Joseph, the writer's father, drove up to the gate at the entrance of the Villa Louis, they met several Indians which were waiting for Dousman to beckon or call them in. Coryer realized this, so he asked the Indians if they were waiting for Dousman to call them in. The Indians answered yes in their language. Coryer then broke the news to them, telling them that Dousman was dead. Some of the Indians said in their language, "Sagga-nash-nepo," and at the same time brought their hands up to their mouths with force. "Sagga-nash-nepo" meant, "Our lord is no more," and some of them wept.*

In the late 1830s or early 1840s, my grandmother's family moved from Montreal, Canada, to Milwaukee, Wisconsin. Their name [was] Hutchinson. My grandmother's name was Eliza. She had two sisters, Minerva and Sarah, and they lived near Lake Michigan. One very warm summer day the girls decided to take their sewing and go down to the lake shore to sew because of the cool lake breeze. There were large trees there which made it shady and also underbrush. The girls picked a spot, sat down, and got busy sewing and chatting as they sewed.

Suddenly they heard something in the underbrush and on looking up they saw several Indian heads looking over the bushes. The girls held their nerve but got up. Just then the leader of the Indians spoke up, "White woman be no 'fraid, me no hurt white woman, my name John."**

In answer Eliza said, "Do you want to eat?"

They answered, "Yes, we hungry."

"Then follow us. We are going home, and Mother will give you food to eat." The Indians did follow them to their home, and their mother gave the Indians food to eat and then they all left satisfied.

My grandfather, Thaddeus Langford, was born in Troy, New York, and left home very young. He worked for a farmer for a few years for his board and clothing just so he could get to go to school, then he worked for the Erie Canal for some time. He there got the understanding of steam and later learned that engineers were in demand in Milwaukee, so he went there and got a job as engineer in a flour mill. After working there for some time he met his wife, Eliza Hutchinson, and they later were married, and a daughter was born to them in 1847, which later became my mother. In 1850, the man which Thaddeus worked for built a new flour mill in Chicago and had Thaddeus move to Chicago to engineer the new mill. The first summer they lived there the cholera epidemic took place, and Thaddeus

---

* Coryer was wrong in his translation. The Indians were not calling Dousman "our lord," but simply "the Englishman." In Ojibwe, the universal language used by fur traders in this region, "Zhaaganaash nibo" translates to "Englishman is dead." John D. Nichols and Earl Nyholm, *A Concise Dictionary of Minnesota Ojibway* (Minneapolis: University of Minnesota Press, 1995).

** The broken English in Coryer's tales probably reflects his stereotypes or efforts to express lack of fluency with English on the part of the Indians more than it does their actual speech patterns.

got it and had it so bad the doctor gave him up as no chance of recovering. Thaddeus was so weak he could barely whisper and he kept asking for water, but the doctor had forbidden Eliza of giving him water. The doctor said it would hasten his death.

And as Eliza was in the house with her dying husband, a knock came at the door and on answering the call she met an Indian woman at the door. She had several baskets to sell, and she asked Eliza if she cared to buy a basket. Eliza answered by saying, "I am sorry I cannot buy. My husband is nearly dead with cholera. The doctor said he could not recover." The [woman] then said, "Can me see husband?" Eliza said, "Yes, if you do not fear getting cholera."

The [woman] answered saying, "Me no 'fraid cholera." She entered and went to where the sick man [lay]. As she came near the bed, Thaddeus asked for water in a whisper. The [woman] understood and said, "He want water."

Eliza answered, "Yes, but the doctor said I should not give him water because it would hasten his death."

The [woman] then said, "Doctor don't know. You want me cure husband?"

Eliza then said, "Yes, if you can do it."

The [woman] took a basin which lay handy, went to the well, and filled the basin with fresh water, and brought it to the bed where the sick man [lay]. Then she asked Eliza to help her to raise Thaddeus's shoulders so he could drink, and she let him drink his fill, then laid him down tenderly. Eliza then thought, if the doctor is right, Thaddeus will soon die now. The [woman] then said, "He get sick now." It was not long before Thaddeus did get sick to his stomach; on helping him he vomited much which was black as could be.

He was very weak and [lay] motionless and speechless for some time. Then he revived and asked for more water, and the [woman] gave him, but he did not drink as much. This time the [woman] said, "He be sick again." She was right, he did vomit again; but this time it was merely colored. He then lay back for some time, then revived and asked for water again which was given him; but he did not drink much this time, and the [woman] then said, "You got meat for broth? He want eat now."

And she was right; it was not long [before] Thaddeus asked for food. The [woman] fed him, giving him broth only for some time.

The [woman] then said, "Your husband get well now, and me go."

Eliza asked the [woman] if she could stay with her until Thaddeus got stronger, and she did stay three days with her. Then she said, "Now me go. Your husband get well fast." She left and Eliza had only five dollars in the house, so she gave it to the [woman] and thanked her and told her to stop in later so she could give her more, but the [woman] was never seen any more.

ANOTHER CURE BY USING ROOTS WHICH INDIANS USED

In the 1850s, logs that were cut in the north woods were rafted down the Mississippi River to sawmills. The men working for those companies received good wages because this work was strenuous and dangerous and when the river froze over so they could not raft down logs, those men would stop over winter in Prairie du Chien, Dubuque, and other places along the river for the winter. Most of them drank and gambled, thereby would get in fights which generally would end by someone being stabbed or shot. Well, there was one stabbed in the chest and the doctor tried to heal the wound which was deep in the lungs full length of the knife blade; and the man grew weaker and thinner and the wound did not heal. The man also was penniless. The doctor gave him up to die, and a Mrs. Limery living in Frenchtown had learned from the Indians how to use herbs and roots. She felt confident she could heal this man, so she had him brought to her home, and she healed the man in time.[24] So he went back to work at his work as usual.

Now to heal him she used a root called spikenard.[25] She got the fresh roots and merely scraped the outer bark off, then sharpened them pencil fashion and stuck the roots as far as possible in the wound and turning the root occasionally, and using fresh roots often this caused the wound to heal from the bottom out.

THE STORY OF HOW, WHEN AND WHERE THE FIRST BUILDING BRICK WAS MADE AND BY WHOM

[It was] about noon on a spring day... Julian Coryer's son Joseph was now fourteen years of age and (as Joseph was born in the year 1845) the year this happened would be 1859. As they came in from the field where they

ADELAIDE LIMERY

Albert Coryer provided additional information about Adelaide Limery's healing methods in his interview with Florence Bittner:

The roots are about the size of a man's little finger. And she'd shape them on the end...how you'd sharpen a lead pencil, so that she could send this down into the man's side as far as the knife had gone. And she did this with this man; and she'd leave the root long enough, out, so that he could turn it. And she told him to turn this root about every fifteen minutes, to...give it a quarter of a turn or so. She kept doing this and in a few days, of course, she didn't have to have such a long root. It had healed from the bottom. And it went on and on till finally, well, the hole was shorter and shorter—the roots had to be shorter and shorter, till finally she couldn't put any more roots in the sore so she formed a poultice and put on the outside, which healed it entirely. The man got stronger and went to work on rafts. And in the fall of the year, he came back after he had worked and saved his money, and he gave Mrs. Limery two hundred dollars and thanked her very much for what she had done....

She used to get my father to go with her and gather roots, different kinds of roots, barks, seeds, berries for different ailments.... And there [are] also a few other roots which are very good, and barks, that I learned through my father, which he learned from her. There is the slippery elm bark, the red elm or the slippery elm bark, that's the inner bark. By steeping this and drinking the tea from this, will cure hiccups, the worst forms of hiccups. And then there is the colt's foot root, which is very good for mouth trouble, if a person has sore gums...or lips, by chewing this root and having the strength from the root go to the affected part, it will cure it. And there were many other ... kinds of roots and seeds and berries that were very good for such as that, that the Indians used, and of course thereby they were their own doctors.

had been sowing grain and had come in to eat their noon meal, they found a stranger at the house waiting for them. As they came in he introduced himself in the French language, his name Mr. La Mee. He had immigrated from France, and he was a brick maker. He asked Julian if he could sample the subsoil to see if it was fit to make brick with, and Julian agreed to let him do so. Julian invited him to eat with them. He appreciated the meal very much. After lunch Julian took him where he realized the subsoil would be fit for brick making, and as the stranger analyzed it, it proved to be satisfactory. He then asked permission for making brick there, telling Julian he would have the job of delivering the brick wherever it was to be used for building and then [because] Julian had good horses and wagons, this was suitable to him. Mr. La Mee also boarded with Coryers whilst making brick.

Now the soil was taken off clean to the subsoil on a few square rods. Then a fence was built of rails tight enough to hold hogs around the space which had been cleaned off. Then La Mee bought a few bushels of corn; then the subsoil was spaded up to a depth of twelve inches. Then water was carried from [the] spring, and the subsoil which had been spaded up was well soaked. And then the corn was scattered on the soaked subsoil. Then La Mee got hogs from Coryer and others and turned them in [the] enclosed area. The hogs got busy tramping and rooting up the subsoil so as to get the corn to eat and by so doing they mixed and prepared the subsoil to [so that it became] mud fit for to put in the wooden forms which had been made to form the brick.

To Show You How Easy It Was to Prepare to Be a School Teacher in District Schools in the Early 1860s

My mother Malvina Langford came to Crawford County, Wisconsin, from Chicago in the year 1854, and she had been attending school two years in Chicago which gave her a start in the district school which she attended about one and a half miles from her home. And when she reached the age of fourteen years and at the end of the school year her teacher, Abbie Hayden, told Malvina that she should apply for a teacher's certificate and go teaching because she was as far advanced in education as she was. So Malvina told Miss Hayden that when she was going to Rising Sun to be

THE BRICK MAKER

Albert continued the story of the brick maker in his interview with Florence Bittner.

MR. CORYER: After this was all well mixed, he drove the hogs back where they belonged, and he had already forms made for making brick, and he used this mud and dried the bricks and then made a kiln, or oven, for cooking the brick, and then inside he piled the brick, filled the oven, with the bricks before they had been baked. And then started a strong... big fire, a very hot fire, and baked those bricks. And they really did make good bricks. He made thousands of them, and they were sold. Several of the main buildings in Prairie du Chien which are now [in 1951] standing are made of those bricks. The Dousman Block and also the creamery building are made of those bricks, and other buildings around Prairie du Chien, and...the only two brick buildings in Frenchtown are made of this brick.[26] And other buildings also. Then later on they started another brickyard at Nickerson's, which, of course, sort of run Mr. La Mee out, and he quit making brick and bought himself a tract of land and went farming....

MRS. BITTNER: I see; and how did they transport this brick from up on the farm down into the town?

MR. CORYER: Now with horses and wagons. They considered one thousand bricks a load. My father and grandfather each had a team and they hauled those with wagons, in wagon boxes.

When [Mr. La Mee] located here, there was not a building where the Village of Eastman now is. The spot was known or called "at the Corners" as there were four corners where the roads crossed. Sometime later, someone started selling groceries here. Then they established a mail route from Prairie to Mt. Sterling. The mail was transferred with horses and a post office was set up here so it was named Batavia. It went by this name up to about the year 1900 when it was found out that there was another Batavia in Wisconsin, which had been named earlier than this Batavia. The state ordered this village to be named different, so it was named Eastman.

NOW AS TO JULIAN CORYER'S WAYS

From Coryer's manuscript "The Life of Julian Coryer"
Julian was of a cheerful nature, always willing to help another if it was possible for him to do so. As soon as his means permitted him to do so he built quite a large frame house, for although his family was small the house was always full of those that needed a place to stay.

Julian and Mr. Henry Prew were the first to get the first grain threshing machine in this vicinity.* At [that] time Julian and his son Joseph owned twenty . . . of the best horses to be raised. If any of the neighbors needed a horse they knew where to go to get one.

After all of Julian's travels in the wilderness, he never forgot his religious training, and in his last years of his life he taught the children of his neighborhood their Catechism. He still had his old Catechism and had it memorized.

Julian also hauled rock to finish St. Gabriel's Church. The church had a start when Julian and his wife settled here, but the builders [ran] out of rock for building it and had to stop until more rock was hauled. Those settlers which had oxen and wagons, time, and goodwill hauled rock, and then enough rock had been hauled; the stone masons also donated their time and labor in building St. Gabriel's Church until it had been completed so the roof could be built over it.**

When Julian and his wife [came] to Prairie du Chien, the missionary priest Father [Joseph] Cretin came or rather stopped over on his way going up or down the Mississippi valley. Mass was then said in private homes, mostly at the Gremore [Grimard] home.*** The [Grimard] home was located in the north end of Frenchtown near [Grimard] Lake as it is called; the proper name for this lake is Courtois Lake. . . . Now when

---

* Henry Proulx was a relative of Julian Carriere and purchased land from the Carrieres in 1858.

** In 1836, Euphrosine Antaya and Strange Powers donated land for the construction of a church. The building of the church, designed by Rev. Samuel Mazzuchelli, OP, took many years to complete. St. Gabriel's Church is the oldest church building in Wisconsin.

*** The name Grimard became known as Gremore, and the lake bore the name Gremore Lake.

continued on next page

Father Cretin officiated at Mass in Mr. [Grimard's] home, Mr. [Grimard] officiated as altar boy or server.*

On one of Father Cretin's stopovers it was arranged to say Mass in the old French cemetery. Mass was said under the large elm tree on the west side of the cemetery. This tree was not large at the time; but gave enough shade to protect the priest whilst he said Mass there.

The Mississippi River was quite high at the time, and a tribe of Indian[s] which were moving north by water in canoes had stopped to rest on the knoll where the old cemetery is. When the Indians noticed the settlers and priest come there, they also came there, so Father Cretin invited and welcomed them to take part at services. And the Indians did so in a very respectable manner and thanked the priest for having welcomed them.

The first building built and used for a chapel was built on the vacant lot north of St. Gabriel's Church. It was also used for school purposes; the building still exists and is used for a dwelling house.** It stands two blocks south of where it was built. It was moved away when St. Gabriel's Church was completed so Mass could be said there and ... what is now St. Gabriel's parish hall was built west of St. Gabriel's convent (which was St. Gabriel's school until the present school building was built). . . . The now called parish hall was moved from where it was built to where it now stands and is now used as a hall when needed for church purposes.

---

* Rev. Joseph Cretin was pastor of St. Gabriel's parish from about October 1841 through April 1844. In 1851, he became the first Roman Catholic bishop of the Diocese of St. Paul.

** This building served as the priest's home and first schoolhouse. The teacher was Miss Denkens while Joseph Coryer attended school.

examined by the county school superintendent which was Mr. William Evans Sr., grandfather of attorney Joseph Evans, that she would go with her to apply for a school to teach if she passed the test.

To go and come back in a day from Eastman to Rising Sun was quite a day for a good team of horses on a light rig. They finally decided to ask a Dr. Foster which was located and practiced about Eastman for his rig to go with. He had a good driving team. On asking him, telling him for what

In 1836, land was donated for a Catholic church at Prairie du Chien. Samuel Mazzuchelli designed the building, and construction began a few years later, requiring many years to complete. The steeple was added in 1889. WHI IMAGE ID 42036

Joseph Coryer and Malvina Langford were married January 17, 1865. PRAIRIE DU CHIEN
HISTORICAL SOCIETY

purpose, he welcomed them to the team. There was quite a stretch of road
that was through the thick woods and occasionally a hold up occurred in
those woods, so Dr. Foster had the girls take his pistol, a one shot, and told
them not to drive too fast before they got to the wood, but on entering
the woods to lay the whip on the horses, and if anyone tried to stop them
to hand them the contents in the pistol. They did as ordered and found
Mr. Evans at home and he gave them the test, and to his surprise Malvina
which was then fourteen years passed higher than her teacher. Mr. Evans
got quite a kick out of that and he gave both of them their certificate for
teaching, thereby Malvina started teaching at fourteen years of age. She
taught up to the age of nineteen; she then married to Joseph Coryer.

PART 2

FRENCHTOWN PEOPLE AND CULTURE

After reading some of Albert Coryer's stories, Florence Bittner informed Ray Sivesind of the State Historical Society of Wisconsin of Albert's wealth of knowledge. Mrs. Bittner invited Albert to her home and in April 1951 interviewed him, basing her interviews on Albert's stories. Sivesind was present as Albert spoke, recording his words as part of a project to record oral histories of pioneers. With many of Coryer's tales, several versions evolved over the years through retellings, and he added even more anecdotes and details during his discussion with Bittner. Most of that interview follows here, with additional excerpts included elsewhere in this book. Sometimes the interview seems more like a conversation, but at other times, Bittner let Albert continue without interruption when he had a lot to say.

When Florence Bittner interviewed Coryer in 1951, he had probably already created his remarkable map of Frenchtown. Drawing in pencil on brown paper, Albert identified all the people who lived along Frenchtown Road from about 1860 to the turn of the century. Beginning at Mill Coulee, Albert sketched the entirety of Frenchtown to Washington Street, depicting the location and ownership of each property with a small detailed sketch of each structure.

His original brown paper map became the basis for yet another illustrated map, now owned by the Villa Louis historic site. It is unclear whether the Villa Louis map was drawn by Albert alone, by another person, or as a collaborative effort. However, the artist was obviously influenced by Albert's stories, by his brown paper map, and other sources. In creating the second map, the artist seems to have been familiar with Lucius Lyon's 1828 map of Prairie du Chien and the 1870 "Bird's-eye View" map of Prairie du Chien published by Ruger & Stoner, pictured on pages 51 and 52. The artist copied the property boundaries and contours from Lyon's map and embellished the scene with steamboats, people of the area, tiny animals, wells, wagons, and islands in the Mississippi River.

Albert Coryer and Florence Bittner may have reviewed his brown paper map of Frenchtown prior to the interview. During the second half of their

49

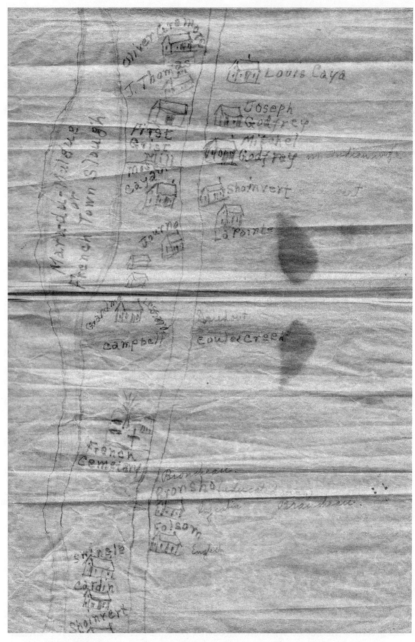

In about 1950, Albert Coryer drew a map of the entire length of Frenchtown Road from Mill Coulee to West Washington Street. He sketched houses in their locations, identifying their ownership or use, and identified the bodies of water that flowed through and west of Frenchtown. DONNA A. HIGGINS

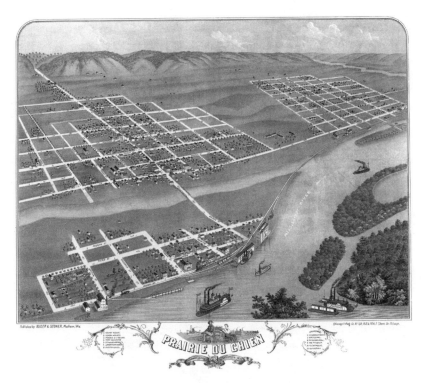

Coryer seems to have been influenced by this map, published in 1870, which showed the three Prairie du Chien neighborhoods south of Frenchtown. WHI IMAGE ID 4111

conversation, Coryer spoke as if he was giving a tour while walking along the main thoroughfare, Indian Trail (a road that would later come to be called Frenchtown Road). Mentally taking a trip down memory lane, he described individually the residents of Frenchtown who lived there in the late nineteenth century. His descriptions correspond to the depictions on the brown paper map, reproduced on page 50, and the later map held by Villa Louis, pictured on pages 54–55. Together the stories and maps combine to create a vivid picture of Frenchtown.

In his interview, stories, and map, Coryer portrayed the residents of Frenchtown fondly and respectfully, sprinkled with gentle humor. This represents a notable change from the ways some Anglo Americans had written about them a century earlier, when prejudice against the French abounded. Anglos and other immigrants often referred to the region's older residents as "half-breeds" or used the terms "Canadian," "French,"

or "Creole" derisively. "The Americans generally consider the Canadians as ignorant," remarked an Italian traveling in the region in 1828. "Whether this be true, I know not; but I do know that I invariably found them very polite and obliging, even among the lower classes."[1] Indian agent and government official Henry Schoolcraft wrote about the French that "it is but repeating a common observation to say, that in morality and intelligence they are far inferior to the American population."[2] The newspapers of Prairie du Chien, written and published by Anglos, rarely reported the activities of Creole residents, but when they did, they created a self-congratulatory triumphalist narrative that reveals much about the editors' prejudices. An article appearing in the *Crawford County Courier* in May 1853, for example, said this about the Creoles: "This class of persons—perfectly destitute of ambition or worthy pride—have been gradually dying out, before the onward march of civilization. . . . Their places have been gradually filled by a healthy immigration; and where sloth, stupor, and vice once ruled, now sturdy farmers, and busy mechanics are instilling a new life."[3] The French Creoles, however, were not dying out, and many of them made their homes in the ethnic neighborhood that came to be known as Frenchtown. Given the level of prejudice in the nineteenth century, the interest that twentieth-century local historians and writers took in this ethnic group represents a real shift in public perceptions among the Anglo majority. Coryer sought to polish the image of his ethnic group and ancestors.

The fact remains that during the time about which Coryer spoke, wrote, and sketched, the residents of Frenchtown were experiencing substantial prejudice from the newcomers and were trying to support themselves with limited access to the fur trade. They employed a number

OPPOSITE: Lucius Lyon surveyed Prairie du Chien and produced this map in 1828. It differed slightly from a previous map done by Isaac Lee. Albert Coryer may have consulted this map to help him make his own map, and he sited it along the shoreline. Like Lyon, who illustrated his map with a few small houses and fences, Coryer sketched the dwellings, stores, boats, and people of the area, even adding tiny animals, wells, and wagons. WHI IMAGE ID 53101

FOLLOWING PAGE: Coryer or an unknown artist created this detailed map of Frenchtown. The drawing was based on the map Coryer drew on brown paper, as well as on Lucius Lyon's 1828 map and the 1870 bird's eye drawing of Prairie du Chien. COURTESY OF WISCONSIN HISTORICAL SITE VILLA LOUIS, PRAIRIE DU CHIEN

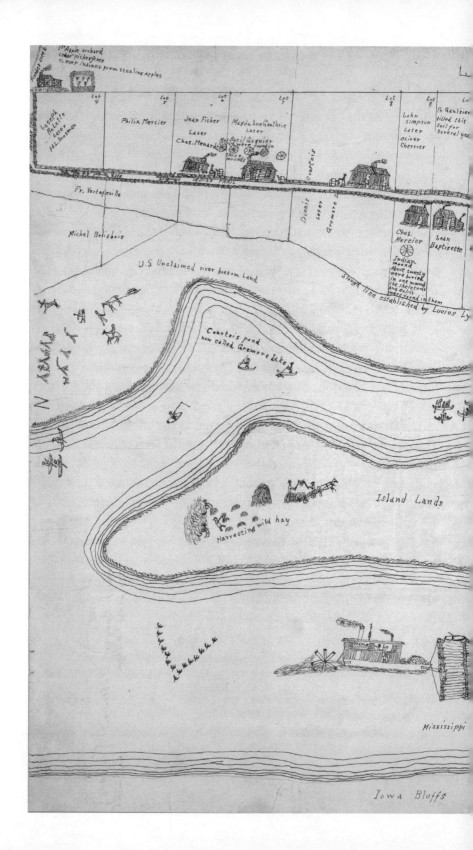

1st Apple orchard
cedar picket fence
To keep Indians from stealing Apples

Lot 4

Lot 5

Lot 6

Lot 7

Lot 8

Lot 9

Lo

Joseph Rolette Later H.L. Dousman

Philix Mercier

Jean Fisher Later Chas. Menard

Magdahne Gauthrie Later
Jos Basil Gagnier were found in 2000 w mounds

Denis Courtois

John Simpson Later Oliver Cherrier

Fr. Gaultier tilled this Soil for Several yrs.

Fr. Vertaflouille

Michel Brisbois

Denis Courtois Later Gremore Jr.

Chas. Mercier

Jean Baptisette

U.S. Unclaimed river bottom Land

Indian mound About twenty were buried in one mound the skeletons and Relics were found in them

Slough line established by Lucius Ly

Courtois pond now called Gremore lake

N

Island Lands

Harvesting wild hay

Mississippi

Iowa Bluffs

Deer were shot here
Salt at the foot of the
tree kept the deer coming

Limery Coulee

Campbell Coulee

Lot 13   Lot 14   Lot 15   Lot 16   Lot 17   Lot 18   Lots 19 & 20

LANE Try's

Campbell estate
Now in the 1860's
owned by H.L. Dousman

Campbell Coulee creek Concession Trout was plentiful here

ling tree here

Louis Stram Brick blk

Louis Caya

Joseph Godfrey

Fred La Pointe

Jean Limery

August Stram

Oliver Gremore

Mitchel Godfrey

Moses Gardepi

Thomas Booth Brick Bldg.

Brick made mill entirely ruined excepting

Moses Caya

Alex. Shoupvert

Ben André

Mary Lessard

of 1858

French town slough

J. S.

Ben. Grant

This is a drawing to give you an idea
of what French Town and the river
was in the 19th Century

low river

of strategies to turn the natural environment into support for their families, and they often relied on each other for assistance, companionship, and mutual aid. Coryer's interview, map, and memoirs provide a variety of information about individuals, the area's changing Native presence, and people's relationships to the landscape.

At the most basic level, Coryer recorded who and what was in Frenchtown in the late nineteenth century. We learn, for example, the locations of the region's first bowling alley and the area's school, which was large enough for thirty children. In addition, Coryer placed the grocery store and the old mill within the community. The detailed drawing suggests the types of architecture of buildings, the location of wells and fences, and the roads along which travelers (represented by tiny people and their tiny wagons and horses) made their way in and out of town. We also learn a bit about the residents. For example, "Limery Lane was named after Mr. John [Jean] Limery . . . the one that first introduced . . . this faith cure here amongst the Canadians, and his wife had learned how to doctor with roots, herbs, and seeds."

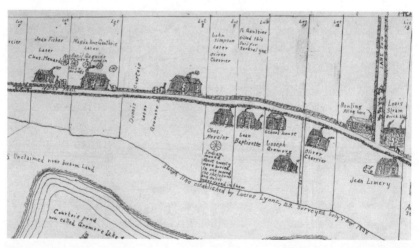

This detail from the Villa Louis map shows the lot numbers copied from the Lucius Lyon map, with residents' names and other details written in. Building details indicate which construction methods were used for each. In lots 6 and 8, residents are depicted using cranks to get water from their wells. In lots 6, 7, and 8, the perspective includes both side- and bird's-eye views, the latter to indicate the presence of Indian mounds. COURTESY OF WISCONSIN HISTORICAL SITE VILLA LOUIS, PRAIRIE DU CHIEN

Coryer's memories not only sketch out the details of the social land-scape of Frenchtown and inform us about the health care available there, but also express continuing relationships with Native people. Here we can find information about the lingering presence of Native people, and about the impact their practices had on local culture. Many of the residents of Frenchtown, such as the Cheneverts, Jeandrons, and Gardepies, descended from the earlier intermarried fur-trade families and had ancestors among the Sauk, Meskwaki, and Menominee tribes. (Coryer spelled their names Shoinvert, Jondro, and Gardipi on the map.) But intermarriage had declined significantly by the mid-1800s, and so Mitchell Godfrey's full-blooded Na-tive wife was unusual enough for Coryer to mention in the interview. The Villa Louis map records Coryer's depiction of Native people as trouble-some outsiders: Coryer describes the "first apple orchard" as having a "cedar picket fence to keep the Indians from stealing apples." On the river and the "unclaimed river bottom land" depicted on the Villa Louis map, however, Indians appear in canoes or near their tents; one is hunting a deer with a bow and arrow, while another leads a horse with a travois* attached. In addition, their historical presence is indicated by the mounds inscribed on several lots, where the artist also included references to excavations.

The main street through town was labeled as "Indian Trail," although on the brown paper map Coryer drew, he labeled it as "French Town Road" with the words "Indian Trail" in parentheses. The name change suggests a shift in the function and usage of the road from one that brought Indians into town to one that took people to Frenchtown. The shift demonstrates a change in Prairie du Chien's collective memory and its concept of out-siders. As the number of Indians coming to town dwindled and people forgot that Natives had laid out the road, newer residents recognized the French Creoles as having an ethnic enclave apart from the center of the village of Prairie du Chien.

In his interview, Coryer described the Courtois family, for whom an Indian presence represented a paranoid delusion. The lingering presence of Native people in the area might have frightened Charles Courtois, but in the local memory, a man so fearful was not in his right mind. The irony,

---

* A travois is a device attached to the back of a horse, comprising a platform between two long poles that were dragged behind. The platform carried baggage and sometimes people.

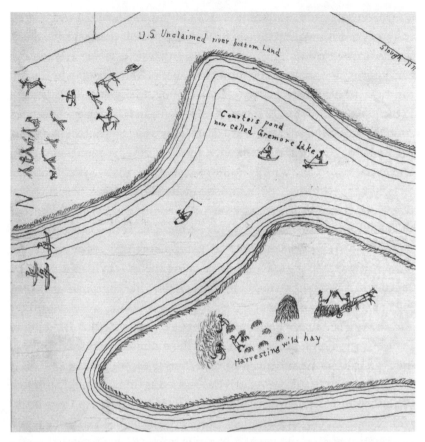

Indians are depicted camping and hunting at the river's edge. The map also shows a tiny deer, a dog, a person riding a horse, and another horse with a travois. Three canoes approach the shore. In the river, one person in a row boat fishes with a pole, while two others in canoes spear fish. (Native and non-Native people on the map seem to use different boat styles, and have different hats.) On an island nearby, five people are "harvesting wild hay." COURTESY OF WISCONSIN HISTORICAL SITE VILLA LOUIS, PRAIRIE DU CHIEN

perhaps, was that both Charles Courtois and his sister, Elizabeth Courtois Grimard, had Native ancestors, probably Menominee.

Frenchtown residents in the late nineteenth century had a keen awareness of the natural environment, and their economy was closely tied to it, in Coryer's stories and the Villa Louis map. The river was among the most important features of the landscape, and of both the local history and economy. More than half of the illustrated map's area covers the Mississippi River, its islands, and the shoreline. Here, we see a steamboat flying American flags and two rivercraft transporting logs to a sawmill somewhere downstream. Coryer's narrative had placed these images in the history and economy of Frenchtown, explaining that his grandfather and great-uncle made money chopping wood for the steamboats. He also mentioned the lumbermen who were unemployed during the winter causing drunken disturbances in town.

Closer to shore, a flotilla of canoes seems to be transporting bundles, perhaps furs. A man in a small canoe shoots birds while another man in a rowboat watches. Two fishermen in canoes spear fish while another in a rowboat uses a pole. The different types of small craft on the map seem to be sorted by Native and non-Native practices: the tiny canoeists appear to be wearing feather bonnets while the other boaters sport other types of hats. This sense of difference extended to fishing practices. Coryer explained in the context of one of his tales that although his father and a neighbor "speared fish by night, . . . Indians would spear fish by day," cutting holes in the ice.

Like the farmers who let their hogs run wild on the islands or shoreline of the river, Frenchtown residents used the uninhabited islands in the way they had used the old common fields of the eighteenth century. The Villa Louis map depicts people "harvesting wild hay" on an island, a practice carried on by Frenchtown resident Mr. Thomas, according to the interview. The uninhabited islands of the Mississippi were resources not only for collecting fodder for cattle, but, according to Coryer's memoir, also provided free range for farmers' hogs. Inland, other resources were also marked on the map: in Limery Coulee, a small person sits in a tree above a tiny deer, with the notation "deer were shot here. Salt at the foot of the tree kept the deer coming." And the creek in Campbell Coulee bears the notation "speckled trout was plentiful here."[4]

In addition to creating a community portrait, Coryer tried to convey a sense of the values of this ethnic group. Albert Coryer said they were "a humble class of people," who, although they were not ambitious, were generous and friendly. This communal theme of looking out for one another and helping the unfortunate comes out in a number of Coryer's stories. (One finds these themes in Anglo pioneers' narratives as well.) But Albert Coryer's anecdotes and yarns were also meant to entertain. Among several funny anecdotes, his last story recounts the efforts of neighbors to assist an elderly couple, only to encounter an unlikely surprise when helping the wife to bathe.

As with any primary source, the map Albert drew on brown paper and his interview and memoir should be used with caution and checked against other evidence for veracity. Many of the details about the residents of Frenchtown can be verified with census data and other records. In addition, his depictions of community values were also expressed in nineteenth-century documents by both insiders and outsiders and have been expressed by descendants in the twenty-first century. Coryer thus shared evidence about the events and economy of the community as well as about the way the community was remembered. These sources provide an important counterbalance to the unflattering newspaper reports and letters written by their newer Yankee neighbors.

FLORENCE BITTNER'S INTERVIEW
WITH ALBERT CORYER

I was born in the town of Prairie du Chien the thirty-first day of August, 1877. I was born on the tract of land which my grandfather, Julian Coryer, bought from Uncle Sam at the price of $1.25 an acre. . . . My grandfather was born at Baye-Saint-Antoine Canada. . . . Now the name is changed to Baye-du-Febvre. It is located south of the St. Lawrence River between Montreal and Quebec. My grandfather's ancestors were some of the first French people that landed in Acadia, which later on moved westward along the St. Lawrence to where my grandfather was born. And at the age of sixteen my grandfather left Canada. He enlisted, or hired out, to the Hudson Bay Fur Company for a period of four years, and they traveled, as the voyageurs did on their old voyageurs' route . . . through the Great Lakes to Green Bay. There they traveled down the Fox River to Portage. Then . . . they . . . carried everything into the Wisconsin River . . . and then down to Prairie du Chien, which was the next place between Green Bay and St. Louis. And as my grandfather left the mouth of the Wisconsin to turn northward, the first white person that he noticed on the riverbank was . . . a lady, . . . the first white woman that came to Prairie du Chien. She was Mrs. Cardinal . . . Her husband was a fur trader—and he had died and she was left alone in their cabin, or log hut; and she had many dogs to guard her which caused my grandfather to take notice of her and the place.

Then they worked on up north, traveled on up north, to the fur trading posts which were located along the riverbank near the Villa Louis. . . . My grandfather said that at that time there were very few people located in the city of Prairie du Chien. All there were were those few along the riverbank, the fur traders and a few other settlers, and then a few settlers along the east side of the slough which forms an island between the river and the slough, and which is part of Prairie du Chien. And then from there, from the trading posts here at Prairie du Chien, the . . . fur company, they went on down south to St. Louis. And there they prepared things, rafts—or

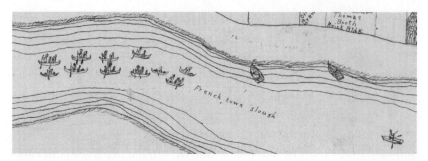

At the Frenchtown slough, this detail shows the residents of Prairie du Chien co-existing with Native people. A flotilla of canoes seems to carry Indians with feathered headdresses. To the right, two empty rowboats are tied up to shore, while at the bottom right, a person with a Euro-American style hat paddles a rowboat. COURTESY OF WISCONSIN HISTORICAL SITE VILLA LOUIS, PRAIRIE DU CHIEN

barges, rather—that they would row by hand, by manpower, they were rowed up the Missouri River, way up to the forts at the source of the Missouri River.... After serving the first four years he enlisted for another four years, and thereby worked eight years for the . . . fur company. And, being tired of this life, he thought he'd settle down and he bought the forty acres of land in what is now part of the city of St. Louis, and built a log house on it, and just as he was about to start farming, the Black Hawk War broke out and they wanted volunteers to serve in this war. So my grandfather, being quite acquainted, and had been amongst the Indians very much, enlisted and served all through the Black Hawk War. After the . . . war was over, he got his discharge; he returned to St. Louis. In a short time he met his wife, Lucretia Lessard, and they were married in the old cathedral in St. Louis.

And shortly after they were married, the terrible cholera epidemic happened in St. Louis and people died by the thousands. But they were blessed and didn't get this cholera, and they said, "Well, now since we were blessed in not having this and dying, we're going to work our way north and get away from those southern diseases." And they worked their way to Dubuque, and there he painted, which he had learned the trade of painting with his father, by helping his father while he was in Canada. And later on, . . . this didn't agree with my grandfather's health, decorating inside. He heard they needed help at the mines at Galena, which were then opening up and they wanted a man and wife, the man to help work in the smelter where they smelted the mineral, and the wife to prepare the meals for the men that worked there. So they moved there and took this job. They worked there awhile and then later on Mrs. Coryer's—my grandmother's—two brothers, John and Frank Lessard, had come from St. Louis on up with a man which trained broncos, or wild horses, tamed them down, trained them, and brought them up towards the north, to the north as far as Prairie du Chien, and sold them to settlers. And they were so taken up with the country about Prairie du Chien they stayed here, and then they came down to Galena and they urged my grandfather and grandmother to come up and buy government land which sold for $1.25 an acre, and farm instead of working in those mines, which they did. And this was about in the year 1840, and . . . about five years, after they were here, my father, Joseph Coryer, was born, 1845, the nineteenth of September.

And then shortly after my grandfather had settled there, his brother-in-law, Frank Gokey, also settled north of him, on the section north of him. And they settled, of course, on those hills. The reason why was they had wonderful water, spring water to depend on, and also timber which they used for building and fuel, and also for fences, because all the fence material they had at the time was rails, rail fences. And that is the reason why those settlers settled up on the hills instead of settling down in the valley. . . .

ON PRAIRIE DU CHIEN'S CREOLE FRENCH CULTURE

Well, the old French settlers were a humble class of people. They didn't try to accomplish very much, but they always had in mind of being generous and friendly to one another, and enjoy themselves. They would help one another whenever it was needed, in case one would get sort of handicapped some way through sickness or hard luck of some kind, get backwards with their work, why, the others would all pitch in and help them. They . . . called this making a bee, getting together and working together. And they'd all get together and fix whatever work . . . should be done so that the other man would be up with his work compared to what the others were. And also the women folks, if the woman . . . of the household would happen to be sick and get backwards with her work and needed help, the women of the neighborhood would all come and help her and get her back to where she should be with her work.

And also as far as enjoying themselves, they were a class of people that tried to be together as much as they could. They enjoyed one another's company, and they would get together especially during the holidays. From New Year's to Ash Wednesday was really the time . . . they enjoyed . . . themselves the most. And they had more time then, of course, because they didn't have to be out in the fields doing so much work outside and they could spend more time in trying to enjoy themselves. They'd start on New Year's Day generally by going to the oldest of the neighborhood, or family, and have dinner with them, and then from there, in the evening, they would go to another older couple, or a house where the people had been living there the longest, and enjoy themselves during the evening.* And from New Year's, then, . . . two or three times a week, they would get together and enjoy themselves by having dances, and songs, and playing cards. The young people would dance, and the older women would get in a room and talk and play cards, and the men, some of them, would get together and sing songs. And to keep themselves up in the right spirit they would have a little alcohol, which was their main drink. They'd dilute it. They'd have a pure grain alcohol and dilute it, half water, and never was any of them drunk. They'd just merely take enough so that, that it'd give 'em pep so that they could enjoy themselves. And . . . about twelve o'clock they'd have a real meal, with nothing missing, you might say. It was a real feast. And after they'd all ate their fill, they'd spend their time from then till two or three o'clock in the morning enjoying themselves dancing, playing cards, and talking and visiting with one another.

And they wouldn't only have the old people there, they would bring the children. The children were brought in the old-fashioned wagon boxes, . . . or the bob sleighs. The box had hay in the bottom and then they would put blankets on this hay and the kids would line up along the edge of the box, and their backs along the sides, and then they were covered with other blankets, and they were taken back and forth in that way. None of them seemed to take sick or catch cold from doing this.

But Ash Wednesday all this was stopped, and the time of Lent began, and they'd devote their time as they should during Lent. And as far as

---

* Albert is describing a French-Canadian tradition. On New Year's Day, social calls were made throughout the community, with due respect given to elders. Elder members of the family are known to bless the children as well as raise a toast to the New Year.

wanting to accomplish very much, as far as earthly gains or laying aside much wealth, it seems none of them tried to do that. They didn't seem to care to do that. All they wanted to do was just live along, have a good time, and not worry. That was the way the old timers wanted to live, or seemed to be inclined to live.

MRS. BITTNER: In other words, the French in those days lived for the good that they could get out of life rather than for material gains.

MR. CORYER: That's right.

MRS. BITTNER: And the French enjoyed singing a great deal in those . . . meetings and at their gatherings.

MR. CORYER: They sure could sing, too. The ladies . . . would get in a room; they'd . . . sing their songs, and enjoy themselves that way.

MRS. BITTNER: Perhaps they were a lot different than the men?

MR. CORYER: They were great people for singing. Of course, the men . . . had what they called drinking songs, but . . . they wouldn't over-drink. . . . None of them would get drunk, but they called them drinking songs because they'd have their occasional little toddy along as they sang.

This is one, just . . . a few words of one of the songs—[singing]

This is the English of it: "The Canadians are no fools. They would never leave without having another drink."

MRS. BITTNER: . . . The houses, the old French houses, up in Frenchtown, that we're going to discuss later on, are rather interesting. The [French-Canadian] houses, are some still in existence up there?

MR. CORYER: Yes; there are still two; and I think probably three, of the old houses still there, or part of them anyhow. . . .

MRS. BITTNER: Could you tell me how they were constructed?

MR. CORYER: Well, they were all [made] of home material; that is, materials that they got out of the woods themselves, parts of trees that they'd hew out and then mortise them together. The studdings weren't as close together as the studdings are nowadays; they'd have them about three feet apart. And then the other pieces that they'd put between the studdings, which was filled with the smaller pieces, were mortised in the sides of those studdings. [They] were about three feet long. And they'd fill this space, between those parts that laid horizontally with the old clay subsoil from the hills, yellow clay, and daubed in there, mudded in there, and then the outside was covered by wide boards. At that time the lumber they got was very good, and they had large trees, and the boards, many of them were as wide as sixteen inches, and which left very few cracks. They were...laid on in a perpendicular way, and then, up and down, and then...they had strips that they nailed over the cracks. That was to prevent the rain or water from washing away this clay, this mortar that they laid between the parts of the wood they had between the studding. And then the inside was plastered real smooth with clay also, and then whitewashed with lime, which made a very nice, white wall, but of course had to be whitewashed twice a year.*

MRS. BITTNER: And these buildings were warm?

MR. CORYER: Yes, they were. Very warm.

MRS. BITTNER: And the floors were what?

MR. CORYER: They were of six-inch lumber, mostly. Just the plain white pine six-inch lumber.

MRS. BITTNER: And they had shingles, or roofing?

MR. CORYER: Well, the very first shingles were ... made right at home. They were made out of oak. They'd saw oak blocks, that is, take large trees and saw them eighteen inches long, the blocks. Then they had a sort of chisel, a knife-fashioned chisel, and they'd lay this chisel on the block and split those shingles so that they could lay them on the roof.

MRS. BITTNER: How were they fastened down?

MR. CORYER: With nails. . . . There was no such thing as a wire nail, . . . They were all square nails in those days.

MRS. BITTNER: The French had a cemetery that was located, and is still located up in what is called Frenchtown at Prairie du Chien. There are

---

* Albert is describing a French-Canadian method of house construction, *pièce sur pièce en coulisse.*

Father Marie Dunand blessed the cemetery in 1817. Until the establishment of St. Gabriel's Cemetery in 1840, this was the only cemetery in the community. MARY ELISE ANTOINE

two. One is the old French cemetery and the other one, of course, is the ... Calvary cemetery.

MR. CORYER: Yes, the old French cemetery is filled with the bodies of all the first old settlers that died here. It's really full. That's the reason why ... they established the other cemetery across the road. Mr. Dousman gave the land for them to establish the other cemetery because this was full. And there [are] very little [few] markers there. There [are] a few plain rocks that mark some of the graves and then the cavities in the ground, where it's caved in. That's all that marks the graves. And then there is one wooden enclosure and that is ... Alexander Gardepie which still is there, has been there as long as I can remember. And there are the two tombs, one of Mr. Rolette—well, first his daughter was buried there and then later Mr. Rolette on the west end of the cemetery. And the settlers fenced this with rock, this plain rock that they got in the hills. It had a pile three feet at the bottom and then brought up to a peak. This was to prevent the cattle and horses from trampling the graves. Finally in about 1890, or such as that, the boys from town would go up around there and they would notice rabbits running under those rocks and they would start tearing down this

Missionary priests and the first two pastors of St. Gabriel's Parish held mass in this building until the stone church designed by Father Mazzuchelli reached a stage where it could be used. MARY ELISE ANTOINE

fence, and then later on the others that needed the rocks for building walls, would go up there and help themselves and now there is hardly any sign of this rock wall.

MRS. BITTNER: You told me a story that your grandfather had told about the burials that took place in the early days in the old Frenchtown cemetery. . . . When the Indians used to come and visit the cemetery.

MR. CORYER: Yes, yes, well . . . that was when they'd say Mass, the missionaries would stop here at Prairie du Chien. The first Catholic priests that came in the valley here . . . were missionaries from St. Louis, at first [to] Prairie du Chien and then later on they went on up to St. Paul. They'd come by Prairie du Chien about once a month.[5] They had no church at the time. That was before the St. Gabriel's Church was built. And in the summertime they would say Mass up in the old French cemetery under a large elm tree. The tree wasn't so large then but it is now very large. And the Indians were most generally camped around this cemetery, which no doubt would understand and know that this priest was coming. When they'd notice the priest come and set up his temporary altar to say Mass, they would all come in, file in as they should, and listen and observe the saying of the Mass as they should, very respectful, and then go away the same way after Mass was over. And my grandmother said that they seemed to realize what was going on very much, by their actions.

FRENCHTOWN PEOPLE

Mr. Coryer: Well, old Frenchtown really started about a half a mile north of the north city limits of Prairie du Chien, and really the first house was right up from the Campbell Coulee Creek. At one time this was a real creek that flowed at the rate of about a foot deep and four or five feet wide. There was a wonderful flow of water there; this was supplied by the springs in the hills in the Campbell Coulee and above the Campbell Coulee. And later this creek went dry and after the Burlington built their road across the Prairie there, why, on account of them building up the dump, the floods from the Campbell Coulee would take—I remember when there was about a quarter of a mile of the dump washed away entirely.[6] They had to build entirely new. The bridge and the dump [were] entirely washed away, on account of the floods from the Campbell Coulee. So the Burlington, to safeguard themselves, dug a ditch from the Campbell Coulee down to the slough which would empty into the river, of course, so that it would be large enough, sufficient to carry this water.

But there is where the old Frenchtown starts. The first house was right north, a few roads north of this ditch, and west of the highway, or the old Indian trail. And this was occupied by my great-grandmother, Mrs. Lessard.[7] She was a widow. Her husband had died in New Orleans. They had moved from Canada down to New Orleans, and on account of so much disease and they didn't like the south so well, they moved back up. Finally they got up to Prairie du Chien. [She] and her son, John, lived there in this house north of this creek.

And just to tell one little incident, or story that happened to her. This was on a winter day, wash day, Monday; she went to the creek where she always got her water. Instead of bringing it up with an open bucket from one of those old dug wells which were reinforced with rock, she would at least rather carry her water from the creek to wash with. And there was sort of a hole, a deep hole, opposite her house, and she cut a hole in the

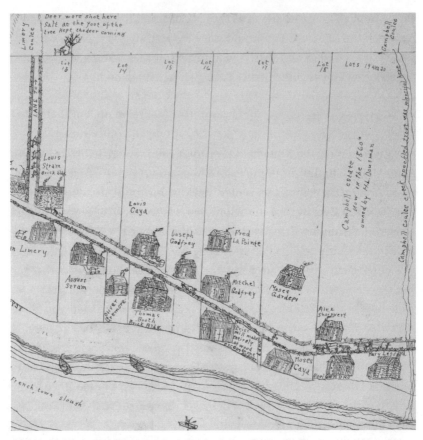

The home of Albert Coryer's great aunt, Mary Lessard, can be seen in the bottom right corner, along Campbell coulee. In the top left is a small sketch of a deer next to a tree with a hunter in it. The text indicates, "Deer were shot here. Salt at the foot of the tree kept the deer coming." In lot 17, a note explains, "Grist mill made entirely of wood except stone hopper." COURTESY OF WISCONSIN HISTORICAL SITE VILLA LOUIS, PRAIRIE DU CHIEN

ice so that she could dip water from that. And as she started to dip her water, every time she'd get a pail out, a pail full of water, there would be two or three fish, small fish, these creek suckers and the like, and of course she would empty her pail out on the ice. And before she could get one pail of clear water to take home, she had about one hundred pounds of fish [strewn] out on the ice; it was just thick with those creek suckers. And well, it's just to say . . . that [shows] the change that has taken place. I am just telling you this just to tell you what change has taken place since then: . . . now, [it is] a dry ditch and [back] then [it was] such a wonderful creek there. And t'weren't only creek suckers, but there were wonderful trout. I know one man [told] me that he shot a trout that weighed three pounds out on the Campbell Coulee. He saw it along the bank, had been out hunting, and he shot it with a shotgun and brought it home, a speckled trout that weighed three pounds.

Now then, there was several houses from there on up, but that didn't last as long as the others north of there, and I can't quite remember of, probably three houses, but the next one was Mr. Jeandron.[8] Mr. Jeandron, he was a man that dealt in horses. He raised a lot of horses. At the time, of course, horses [were] used for pulling streetcars and also altogether on the road; that was the only thing they had for getting around with, and he raised horses. And, of course, the faster the horses were, the better, and the more he could get for them, and the better they'd sell.

And well, his wife died, and then he met a widow which had a son, and this son was great for riding around with the horses, too, and of course, occasionally he'd take a leave of going and taking one of the old man's horses and having a good time riding up and down on the ice during the winter. This man would train his horses on the ice and on Frenchtown slough, which was about half a mile long. . . .

Well, he didn't spend much in raising those horses because those days they had free range. All they had to do in the spring of the year when the grass got good enough so they could pick their living, was to turn them loose, let them go out on the prairie and in the hills. And then all they had to do was get feed for them during the winter. And so that was the way he made his livelihood.

Well then, the next one on the same side of the road, the west side of the road, was Moses Caya.[9] He was a sort of a builder. Really his trade was stonemason. And then across the road, that was between this Jeandron and Caya, there was a Nicholas Chenevert.[10] And then south [north] of him on the east side of the road there was Gardepie.[11] There were two families of Gardepie. Then right near Nicholas Chenevert there was a John LaPointe.[12]

This John LaPointe was the captain, or pilot, on the riverboats. He got his living that way, by working summers on the riverboats. And then right north of them there was the two Godfreys. Mitchell Godfrey first, that's on the east side of the road, Mitchell Godfrey, and he married an Indian, a Fox [woman]. And there [were] three children born to them, two daughters

The Vertefeuille house is the only home remaining of the many Albert located on his map of Frenchtown. In 1854, Moses Caya purchased the house. It remained in the Caya family until 1940. ROBERT CAMARDO

and a son. The [wife] soon got so that she lived the same as the other old settler women there, the French women, dressed and cooked and got along the same as the other women, and spoke the French language, of course. And still, when springtime came, she'd get lonesome for her old way of living with the Indians and also visiting her folks, so she'd just tell Mitchell, "Now, you've got to take care of the children while I go visiting." And she'd just put on her Indian attire and a blanket over her head and away she'd go, and she'd be gone three or four weeks. Then she'd come back to her husband, Mitchell Godfrey.[13]

Well then, the next north of him was Joe Godfrey, and he had quite a strip of land. Probably before I go any further I should describe how this Frenchtown was divided up. On the west side of the road it was divided up in village lots and there were narrow lots. They [ran] from eighty feet to three hundred feet. They were called village lots. They [ran] from the highway, or Indian trail at the time, down to the slough, ... well, wherever the water was. And then on the east side of the road [were] the farm lot lands. And they were divided up in strips, too. They were narrow but they extended from the road to the bluffs. And each man would take about what he thought he could cultivate. And some of them built on the farms. Those built on the east side were built on the farm lots. And their way of measuring their land was the French way. They didn't measure it by acres, it was arpents, A, R, P, E, N, T. Arpent means, comparatively to acre, only . . . there isn't as much land considered in an arpent as there is in an acre.* . . .

Across the road . . . from Joe Godfrey was the old gristmill. This old gristmill was entirely built of wood excepting the two stones that would grind the grain or wheat. Even the cog wheels were made of wood. They had no way of getting any metal materials here in Prairie du Chien at the time and of course they had to use wood altogether, and they had to have a way of grinding their wheat. And this did the old settlers as long as they didn't have a better one. And my father told me, my father was born in 1845, and the way he told me he was just a boy old enough to remember this. [He] and the other boys would go in there and turn those cogwheels and play as boys will. And Louis Dousman II, at times his mother would be visiting up at Frenchtown, and he would be in with the other boys playing in this old mill. And then this was abandoned, this mill, when a man by the name of Gay built the mill where Gays Mills, the village of Gays Mills is now, and . . . the power he used was waterpower, a waterwheel, which was much better and made a better flour, a better grade of flour, too, than this old wooden mill. That was why they abandoned this.

Well, north of this old mill was a man by the name of Thomas. And this man Thomas came in there after the Booths had sold out.[14] They sold out to Thomas. And across the road was Louis Caya.[15] Louis Caya had married a daughter of the Booths that lived there before Thomas did. Well, there is a little story connected with Thomas. This Thomas used to raise horses too, he was a great horseman. And he made his hay, or got his feed from the islands. And there was one time that there was a suitcase full of money lost there in the islands by a couple of robbers. Later on I'll tell you . . . the story about the robbers, but this suitcase was found by this Thomas's hired man. He always had a hired man that worked with him to mow the hay. They mowed it with a scythe. And the hired man hooked the scythe in this suitcase and it seems that Thomas was wise enough to realize what

---

* An arpent was equal to 0.85 acre as a unit of area, or 192 English feet as a linear unit.

this suitcase was. He says when the hired man told him, "Here's an old suitcase." "Oh, yes, this was a suitcase I had here last year and I forgot it here. I had my clothes in there, my extra clothes, sometimes there would come a shower, and I wanted dry clothes to put on and I'll take it." And he takes the suitcase to the wagon.

Well, this Thomas was an ambitious man. He generally worked quite late in the evening and made use of the day as much as he could. But this day he wasn't so anxious in staying there so late. He was anxious getting back home, and about four o'clock he says, "Well," he says, "we did a good day's work today. We're goin' home now." And there was an old frame house or an old-fashioned house that he lived in, and it seemed he didn't seem to have much money either. But after this happened, why, he built quite a good brick house which is still there at Frenchtown and seemed to have plenty of money. So later on you'll find out where this old suitcase come round . . . that [was] dropped in the islands.

Now, next in there was Grimard, Oliver Grimard.[16] He made his living by hunting and fishing, trapping—trapping is really where he made his money, mostly—and also shooting ducks and geese and then selling the meat, the carcasses, to hotels and places in Prairie du Chien and people that didn't go out hunting. And also the feathers—at that time the feathers were worth a whole lot and he made money by that.

And then next to him, on the same side of the road, was August Stram. He came here with his brother, Louis Stram. They came from the Red River district in Canada. Apparently they were some of the first Norsemen that come up in that part of the country, but they had been with the Canadians so much, they spoke the Canadian language. Stram is really not a French name, as you notice, but when you would live with 'em, why, you'd really think that they were real Canadians (which they were Canadians, too, they had been born in Canada), but their ancestors, as I understand, came from Norway or Sweden.[17]

And, well then, his brother lived across the road that was on the east side of the road, Louis. And soon as they could get brick from my grandfather's place, he built a large brick house, and he also built it so that he could keep a store and a tavern on the first floor and lived on the upper floor, the second floor, which he did that for several years, and made money there in that way, and also operated a farm, too. He had a farm lot across from the road to the bluffs.

And then right next to him, that is, across the lane that leads from the Frenchtown Road or the Indian trail to the bluffs, Limery Lane, as they call it, was the old bowling alley. That's the first bowling alley that was ever here in Prairie du Chien, and people would come from miles away to play, to bowl there. And that was quite a thing, till they got one down in Prairie, down on Blackhawk Avenue now, Bluff Street then, down there where the Legion Hall is now, and near there somewhere. Anyhow, then they abandoned this old bowling alley there. I still remember, well, just the old remains of it, a few boards and the foundation. When I was a boy I used to go by there, and I remember that.

Now . . . Limery Lane was named after Mr. John Limery, which lived right opposite, west across the Indian Trail, and he also owned most of the Coulee, the Limery Coulee, and there's where it comes that they called it the Limery Coulee and also the Limery Lane.[18] Now this John Limery is the one that first introduced, or brought about, this faith cure here amongst the Canadians, and his wife had learned how to doctor with the roots, herbs, and seeds. . . . I have mentioned what she could do with her ways of doctoring in the previous recording.

Now next to them on the same side of the road, the west side of the road, was Oliver Cherrier.[19] He was quite a farmer. He owned quite a bit of the land on the east side of the road. And then north of him on the same side of the road was a Joe Grimard.[20] He was the son of the old and first, the first Grimard that came to Prairie du Chien or Frenchtown, and I'll mention his name later. And on this Joe Grimard's land was the first schoolhouse that was built there at Frenchtown. It was . . . an old-fashioned house with those boards, up and down wide boards with cleats nailed to it, and it was large enough to accommodate about thirty children. And of course an old box stove. I went to that school myself just a few years. I finished the district school, what I could learn in district school, there myself.

And then north of this was Baptisette, an old man and his son that lived there. Well, I suppose the old lady, or the mother of the son, was living at one time there, but the reason why I mention this—the son had gone to town one day and apparently the old man had—it was late in the fall, it was

A school on Frenchtown Road was built in about 1859 on land belonging to Joseph Gremore. In the fall of 1885, Albert and his sister and brother started attending classes in the Frenchtown School. In 1900, a red brick structure replaced the original building and was used as a school for twenty-seven years. WHI IMAGE ID 10731

getting quite cold, and the old man had built quite a fire in the stove, . . . and none of them had any brick chimneys, they just had a stovepipe going through the roof and it was a piece of tin around it. And the roof had got afire, and someone that just happened to be going by noticed the roof flaming, and so they run in and told Mr. Baptisette that his house, or his roof, was afire. "Oh, is it?" he says, "Well," he says, "Charles is gone to town. And when he comes back, I'll tell him." He says, "He'll put it out." Of course, the people that [had] seen this realized that when Charles would come, why, there wouldn't be any house there, it would be all burnt, so they got water from the well, and they put the fire out.

Well then, next to him on the west side of the road was the old man, Mr. Grimard, the father of Oliver and Joe Grimard which I have already mentioned. And he owned quite a patch of ground there, and it also extended to Grimard Lake.[21] And this land that he owned was really gotten through a man by the name of Courtois, Charles Courtois, and of course Grimard married this Charles Courtois's sister, and this Charles Courtois had gone daffy, or insane, it seems, so that . . . all he'd done was walk up and down the Sandy Ridge around Grimard Lake, with a club in his hand, chasing Indians away. He said he was protecting the place from Indians. Of course the Indians could soon have made away with him if they'd wanted to, but it seems they realized they shouldn't. (Well, the government, of course, they feared the government. They'd been after them.) And the Indians never bothered him, but he just imagined he was the one that was keeping the Indians away. . . . Grimard, of course, then through the marriage, . . . got possession of this land, but this Courtois really was the one that the name of Grimard Lake was first brought about.[22] It wasn't Grimard Lake, it was Courtois's Pond, and then later on it took the name of Grimard, because of course Grimard owned the land there.[23]

Well then, that just about ended the village lots and the small places. And then next was Basil Gagnier, and he also . . . farmed quite a bit, and then there was . . . the Menard family.[24] And well, really there was two Gagniers, and they all lived . . . between the Mill Coulee and Grimard Lake.[25] They each had a patch of ground and they lived there. Well, that about ended the Frenchtown as far as the Mill Coulee Creek. That's about as far as they went, where the Mill Coulee Creek flowed to the river.

Well then, next and the last was Mr. Chenevert *Le Gros*. *Le Gros* means the French word for "the big" . . . meaning the Big Chenevert.[26] He was a large, strong man, and to distinguish him from the other Chenevert, they, well, they'd say the Big Chenevert and anyhow, this Mr. Chenevert—this was along in the spring of the year—[was] in the house one morning and he heard a rap at the door, and he went to the door and there [were] two men, strange men. And they asked if he wouldn't let them in so that they could dry their clothes by the fireplace. And Mr. Chenevert, of course, let them in and they hurried to the fireplace and took their coats off and put them where they could dry, and then they scattered the contents of a satchel, a large satchel—which I mentioned before where this Mr. Thomas's hired man had hooked the scythe in, well, apparently this is the satchel. But anyhow, this satchel was full of greenbacks, or paper money, and they spread this on the floor. They were all wet; this money was all wet, so they spread that on the floor in front of the fireplace so that it would dry. And one of them kept a close watch towards Prairie, south, looking south all the time, looking out the window. And . . . Mr. Chenevert *Le Gros* noticed

Brothers Theodore Chenevert and Fred Chenevert are pictured at the house probably built by their father. It was demolished after Theodore's death in 1945. It was located on the east side of Frenchtown Road across from Moses Caya's home, now known as the Vertefeuille house. MARY ELISE ANTOINE

that and thought there must be something wrong, he suspicioned there was something wrong, and he asked no questions, of course.

And suddenly the man that was looking out the window says to the other, "Pick it up, pick it up, they're comin'," and they both hurried and picked the money up and jammed it down into the suitcase, the satchel, and closed it, grabbed their clothes, and opened the window on the north side of the house, they went through the window on the north side of the house, and out of the window they went with the satchel.

And of course Mr. Chenevert knew then just about what had happened, that they were thieves and crooks of some kind. And so he went and looked out the window, and there he saw a rig, a light rig with one horse hooked to it, and apparently two officers riding in the rig. And so he stepped out of the house and those men drove up to the house and they asked Mr. Chenevert if he hadn't seen two strange men that morning about there, so Mr. Chenevert as quick as he could told them all about those two that had come in his house and how they had disappeared through the window. So the officers told Mr. Chenevert to take care of the horse and they both got out and ran . . . towards the lake, Chenevert Lake (there is a lake there that is named after Mr. Chenevert). And of course Mr. Chenevert said they had gone down towards the lake. And before the officers got there, the two thieves had just about [swum] the lake. They were on the other side, and they shot at them with their revolvers they had there, . . . but they were right near the willows and they disappeared in the willows. But later on it was thought that they must have hit the one that was carrying the satchel, when they shot at him, and of course, the body floated and the satchel went down. And that was the satchel that was found by Mr. Thomas and brought home that afternoon. And that just about ends Frenchtown.

I'm sorry but I forgot . . . one old party that lived in Frenchtown, and really the most important. That was the old Baptisette family. They lived right north of Joe Grimard's, and they were the oldest couple at that time, I guess anytime, in Frenchtown. The old lady was supposed to be 140 years old.* She was once Mrs. Cardinal, the first French woman that landed here in Prairie du Chien, or about Prairie du Chien, and she'd been married four times. Mr. Baptisette was her fourth husband and of course he was much younger. He was a young man compared to her. He was past eighty and he still made the living for the two of them. He would work around for the neighbors on the farms and also did some trapping and some hunting, and they made a living.

But one spring it was . . . getting on towards house cleaning time, and they realized the old lady couldn't very well clean her house herself, so the ladies of the neighborhood, and those that knew her, got together—my mother was one of them—went there, and they cleaned house for her. The house was in terrible condition, of course. And then finally they said they'd give the old lady a bath, and on giving her a bath, they found that she really had moss growing on her back, that there was sort of a mossy formation there couldn't be washed away—it was on the order of plush and of course the old lady lived a short time afterwards, so she was really over 140 years old when she [died].

---

* Of course, Mrs. Cardinal did not live to be so old, but she did live a long time. Mrs. Cardinal's supposed one hundred forty years became part of the local folklore, as is evident in Albert Coryer's retelling.

PART 3

A VOYAGEUR'S WORLD

After retiring from forty-five years of living on the family farm, Albert began a habit of telling his niece and nephew the stories of his grandfathers that he had heard as a boy. At the urging of family members, he wrote down the stories he remembered about Julian Carriere and Thaddeus Langford to preserve them for future generations. He called the collection "The Grandson of Two Runaway Granddads." He recorded the stories in a 1931 daily memorandum book that had been given out as a form of advertising by the Otto Insurance Agency in Prairie du Chien. The stories revealed that both of Albert's grandfathers had left home at an early age. While Julian had many adventures as a voyageur and employee in the fur trade, Thaddeus worked on farms, moving west from New York to the Midwest.

Several years later, Albert rewrote the stories about Julian Carriere, filling over one hundred pages of loose-leaf paper. He placed the narrative in a three-ring binder and gave it to Florence Bittner, the former curator of the Villa Louis historic site. Lacking a title, Albert wrote, "This is a short sketch of the truthful incidents of the life of Julian Coryer written by his grandson Albert Coryer." Mrs. Bittner's questions for Albert indicate that she probably had read these stories before her interview with Albert.

The stories Albert recorded for his family began with a very personal anecdote in which Albert compares himself to his two grandfathers. In all of Albert's writings and in the interview with Mrs. Bittner, this is the only comment Albert made about his own life. Like his two grandfathers, as a young man Albert had sometimes wished to leave home for an adventure. Referring to himself in the third person, Albert wrote:

The writer or grandson was inclined to leave home and desired going for himself; but because his father lost his health and could not provide as he should, Albert stayed at home and helped his parents up to their death. The parent[s] were kind to him and tried to do all they could for him; this convinced him that he should stay by his parents. For instance when the Spanish-American war was declared, Albert desired

Julian Carriere, circa 1845-1850. PRAIRIE DU CHIEN HISTORICAL SOCIETY

to enlist; but on mentioning this to his parents, his mother said, "Don't you think we need you here at home more than Uncle Sam does?" Therefore Albert stayed at home and worked to keep up the home.

Julian died when Albert was five years old. Julian's wife, Lucretia, continued to live with their son Joseph and his family until her death in 1901. Even though very young, Albert may have picked up on some of the stories that Julian had told of his life in the fur trade. Most likely, these recollections were reinforced over time by Lucretia and Joseph, with Albert listening intently as the family stories were told and retold. How detailed the original telling was when Julian narrated and was asked to recount the adventures he experienced before his marriage to Lucretia will never be known. In the years that succeeded Julian's death and the retelling of his stories by people who had not experienced the fur-trade life, some facts were lost and others narrated in terms of the personal knowledge of the reteller.

For all of his life, Albert remembered the tales he had heard of Julian's long trip by water from Quebec to Prairie du Chien and down the Mississippi River to then venture farther west and travel up the Missouri River onto the open plains. Relishing the tales of travel by water, the hardships Julian withstood, and the encounters with Indians, Albert would tell and retell his grandfather's adventures. These stories Albert remembered and recorded contain great details about the difficult and arduous life of a voyageur in the fur trade west of the Mississippi River. "Voyageur" is the French word for traveler. In the fur trade, it refers to the contracted employees who worked as canoe paddlers, bundle carriers, and general laborers for fur-trading firms from the 1690s until the 1850s. Voyageurs were also known as "engagés," a French term that loosely translates to employees, as they signed a contract, or engagement, to work for a specified length of time in a defined trading region.[1]

The stories recorded by Albert are rich with information on the life of a voyageur in the western fur trade. The tales document the daily life of these men, working in all weather conditions, forced to hunt to supplement their basic provisions, always considering whether their encounters with Indians would be friendly or tense, and never quite sure of the honesty of their fellow engagés. It is a rare source of information on the life of the ordinary, often illiterate men, who were the workers and bore the hardships of the fur trade.

Albert's narratives contain no dates, but his recounting of events, combined with historical documents, have made it possible to determine dates and set some of the stories in context. Julian Carriere was baptized in l'Acadie, Quebec, in June 1813, the son of a laborer, Denis (Louis) Carriere, and Marie Caron.[2] Acadians had established the village of l'Acadie after their expulsion by the British from Acadia during the French and Indian War. Acadia was a colony of New France in northeastern North America that included parts of contemporary eastern Quebec, the Maritime

Provinces of Canada, and Maine to the Kennebec River. In the twenty-first century, the village of l'Acadie is part of St. Jean-de-Richelieu, a few miles southeast of Montreal. For reasons Albert relates, at the age of sixteen Julian left his family and engaged at Montreal to work in the fur trade.

In 1830, Gabriel Franchere, an agent for the American Fur Company, was active in Montreal, signing up young men to work in the fur trade on the Missouri River. From the end of March until the first of May of that year, Franchere recruited at least fifty-five young men from the villages around Montreal. Each signed an engagement to work in "Dependances des Etats-Unis, Haut-Canada, Riviere Missouri, Michilimackinac." Most of the engagements were for a period of three years.[3] While the name "Julian Carriere" is not one of the fifty-five, there is a "Julien Lazure" who signed an engagement of three years to work for the American Fur Company in the Missouri River fur trade. This may have been Julian Carriere using another name because, as Albert related, Julian was running away from home.

Though Albert did not give names to all of the rivers, as did others in the fur trade, Julian would have traveled the St. Lawrence River and the Great Lakes to Green Bay and then down the Fox-Wisconsin waterway and up the Mississippi River to Prairie du Chien. After a brief stop at the Prairie, Julian and the men with whom he traveled would have continued down the Mississippi to St. Louis and then up the Missouri River to "the fort."

In 1832, when he was either between engagements or taking a short leave from the American Fur Company, Julian volunteered to serve in the Black Hawk War. He enlisted under yet another name, according to a bounty land warrant he received in 1855 based on his Black Hawk War service. The patent for the 160 acres stated "Julien Carriere Corporal, who served in the name of Zelo Corey in Captain Geer's Company, Illinois Militia, Black Hawk War."[4] Under this name, Julian enlisted in the Twenty-Seventh Regiment of Illinois Militia on May 27, 1832. After the battle of Stillman's Run, Governor Reynolds had issued a call for more men to protect Illinois. Captain Hezekiah H. Geer of Galena had formed a company and began to enlist men on May 15. Geer's company was one of eight companies recruited from Jo Daviess County that was to protect Galena. After an uneventful summer, the men were all mustered for discharge on September 6, 1832.[5]

After his discharge, Julian apparently returned to St. Louis. There, according to family tradition, Julian met Lucretia Lessard. Julian and Lucretia were married on June 13, 1836, in the Catholic Church.[6] Julian may have spent the years between the end of the Black Hawk War and his marriage working in the fur trade or in one of the other endeavors Albert describes. He had definitely returned to the fur trade for employment by the time of his marriage, as company records indicate he worked in the fur trade from 1836 to 1838.[7]

After Julian completed his engagements in the fur trade, he and Lucretia began to move toward Prairie du Chien. A man known as J. C. Carriere lived in Carrollton, Illinois, in 1840. Based on the ages, ethnicities, and occupation—listed as agriculture—recorded in the US census for the household members, this may have been Julian and Lucretia.[8] In 1842, Julian lived in the Eastern Division of Grant County, Wisconsin Territory.[9] Three years later, Julian and Lucretia had moved to the Town of Prairie du Chien, where their son was born in September 1845. At this point Julian told the census taker that he was engaged in farming with Oliver Carriere.[10]

As Albert stated in his introductions to "The Grandson of Two Runaway Granddads" and the later manuscript written on loose-leaf paper, what he wrote "was truthfully told by Julian himself to his wife Lucretia and his son Joseph, which was handed down to Albert the writer." Albert was therefore recording stories of events that had occurred a hundred to a hundred and thirty years before. By his own statement, Albert had heard the stories second- and thirdhand. In the course of the telling and retelling, some facts had gotten blended, relocated, changed, or lost. French names had acquired English translations. And events that Julian had heard about or learned from others became attributed to Julian and part of his life experiences.

Albert made a few understandable mistakes regarding Julian's work. When Julian had reminisced about his work in the fur trade, he must have used the term "the Company" to identify his employer. By the mid-twentieth century, the major and best-known fur-trading company still in existence was the Hudson's Bay Company. Albert apparently assumed that Julian had been engaged as a voyageur for the Hudson's Bay Company and added that errant detail to his stories. It is more likely that Julian initially engaged to work for the Western Department of the

American Fur Company. Later Julian worked for Pratte, Chouteau and Company, headquartered in St. Louis, which had purchased the Western Department of the American Fur Company in 1834. With Pratte, Chouteau and Company, Julian worked in both the Sioux Outfit and the Upper Missouri Outfit in 1836, and the Sioux Outfit in 1837 and 1838, according to company records.[11]

Albert also seems to have been confused about where Julian used different kinds of boats. In journeying from Montreal, Julian would have helped paddle a canoe, ridden a keelboat, and oared a flatboat. But in his stories, Julian must have mentioned the Missouri River "bull boats," which had frameworks made of willow branches bent in a huge bowl shape with buffalo hides stretched around the framework with the fur on the outside. Bull boats, designed and first used by the Mandan Indians, were used only on the upper Missouri River and its tributaries, but Albert assumed they were used on the rivers east of St. Louis.

Coryer includes several stories about the voyageurs' encounters with Indians. These take a different tone from those in his other writings, seeming to reflect both the tensions between Indians and Europeans that existed in the 1800s and the racial stereotypes that were prevalent when Albert was recording this set of stories in the mid-twentieth century. Some of the anecdotes about Indians are clearly fictional or distorted, and Coryer uses the derogatory term "savages," copying the stereotyped and racist language of movies and other popular media of his time.

As recorded in the two manuscripts, the stories about Julian's adventures in the fur trade and experiences before he began farming at Prairie du Chien are close to identical in their retelling. The same stories are narrated almost word for word and follow one another in the same order. Periodically, Albert included a small detail in one version that he had not recorded in the other or rephrased aspects of the story. These slight variances did not substantially alter each tale. Mrs. Bittner in her interview of Albert probed to learn more, and again, once in a while Albert recollected a small aspect to add to the story. It is obvious from reading the two manuscripts and listening to the interview that Albert told all that he remembered of the stories about Julian that he had listened to as a boy.

The stories narrated in "The Grandson of Two Runaway Granddads" may have been the first time Albert wrote down what he remembered of

Julian Carriere's early adventures far from Prairie du Chien. That manuscript therefore was used as the basis for this chapter. When the loose-leaf Bittner voyageur manuscript and the Bittner interview provide additional information and details, these have been included, with their sources given in the endnotes.

What Albert learned and recalled of the life of Thaddeus Langford before his arrival in Crawford County, Wisconsin, was much less detailed. Thaddeus experienced no great adventures on the frontier, and his rural life was similar to that of other farmers. By the year of Albert's birth in 1877, Thaddeus and Eliza Langford had left Wisconsin for Michigan. Albert remembered a few accounts told to him by his mother when the Langford family had resided in Eastman Township. Though a part of "The Grandson of Two Runaway Granddads," most of these recollections Albert later incorporated into "Short Stories Handed Down" and are related in previous chapters.

The Julian Coryer Stories

Julian "Carriere" Coryer was born in Canada in the village of La Bay du Fave located between Quebec and Montreal in the year 1813. His parents were descendants of the first French people to land in Canada. Julian was the eldest of a family of twelve children.[12]

His father was a painter and earned his living and the living of his family by painting and decorating buildings. When Julian was twelve years of age his father kept him from school to help him with his work. Julian was a faithful worker and helped his father a great deal by cleaning the surfaces, which his father painted. His father was well pleased with him. And when Julian reached the age of sixteen the father realized his son should have a horse to go about with his friends to parties about the parish.

So Julian was very much surprised and happy when he was told that he would have a horse of his own because he had been a good son and helped his father much. The father had three horses but only one cart and harness until they could get another outfit. So he told Julian he could use his outfit until they would get another.

Julian was delighted.[13] It happened there was a party in the adjoining parish. He knew of a few of his friends who were also invited.[14] So Julian invited his friends to gather at his place, and he would take them to the party with his horse and his father's outfit. Julian had told his father his intentions of taking his friends to the party.*

So he thought it would be okay to use it when the time came. The time came, and the friends arrived. So Julian harnessed his horse and was about to hitch it to the cart. And Julian's mother was expecting to be sick at any time and would need help, but Julian did not realize this. Then Julian's father noticed Julian was about to hitch the horse to the cart. Julian's father did not consider what it meant to Julian.[15] He came out and said, "Julian,

---

* In this context, "outfit" refers to a bridle, straps and bands, and cart. Julian owned a horse but had to borrow these items from his father. In the Bittner voyageur manuscript, Coryer said that he told his father about the outfit he intended to use, but not about his plan to take his friends to the party.

put that horse back in the barn. I will be needing it soon myself." Julian obeyed at once, but it grieved him much.

After putting everything to its place, he sorrowfully said to his friends, "Well, friends, I am very sorry to disappoint you and very much grieved to think that after father had given me the horse and told me I could use his outfit as he did, then at the last minute go back on his word and speak to me so harshly. I am telling you that I have made up my mind never to touch the horse or outfit again. I do not care to go to the party tonight. Please forgive me and go and enjoy yourselves without me."

They all said, "No, you must come with us. It is not far, and we can walk there easily." He finally consented and went with them. But he did not take part in the dances or games.

He spent the evening in meditation of what to do. He did not want to see his father again. He had grieved him too badly.[16] He was sorry to leave his mother and planned to see her again. He knew that the Hudson Bay Fur Company* wanted young men to enlist with them to go west in the United States and Canada, so it struck him he would enlist and go with them. But they would not be leaving before two or three days. And where would he stay until then. He decided to ask one of his young friends, which was present at the party, if he could hide out in their barn and wait for the expedition to start. His friend agreed to the plan and also told Julian that he would bring him food and drink, so he would not suffer whilst in hiding.

Julian then went to the Hudson Bay Fur Company and enlisted for four years. When the time came for the expedition to start, he returned to his home to bid his mother goodbye, knowing his father would be away from home. He found his mother in bed with a newly born baby boy by her side. On seeing this, Julian realized why his father had acted as he had the evening he had stopped him from using the rig.

His mother explained everything to him and begged him to stay. But he had enlisted and now he must go. He kissed his mother, brothers, and sisters good-bye. It was his last good-bye to his mother for he was never to see her again.

---

* This was the American Fur Company, which had a recruiting office in Montreal beginning in 1816.

Julian Starts His Adventures

Julian went to the company headquarters on the St. Lawrence River bank. It was a bright fall morning, and the river was calm. A large barge with ten huge oars on each side was waiting. And the men were waiting for the orders to start. The older men greeted him, calling him "young fellow" and telling him right then that he was starting a hard job. He realized it and began to feel sorry for what he had done in anger, but it was too late. His father did not try to find him when he did not come home from the party. He realized he was no doubt pouting over what had happened. And he thought he would come home when he learned what had happened— that he had another baby brother. So he just let him go, never imagining he had enlisted in the Hudson Bay Fur Company. The order to start was given, and the twenty men were stationed at the oars, one man at the stern and one at the bow to be on the lookout for obstructions, which might be in the way or Indians that might be waiting to attack them as they passed by.

This man would sing French songs in a low tone. And the men at the oars would act in harmony with the oars. Julian was stationed at an oar. His hands were tender and not too strong, because he had not done [this] heavy work before. He was the youngest of the band. The day was long with only a stop to have a drink of water and lunch at noon or thereabout. The food was not very appetizing, but he was hungry and made the best of it.

Night came and a suitable place was spotted to camp. A blanket was all they had to wrap themselves in, and it serve as a bed, also. Two men kept watch whilst the others slept, changing every two hours. At dawn, they broke camp and proceeded on their journey up the St. Lawrence River to the Great Lakes.[17]

Going back to the manpower. Julian said they changed positions every half hour, so that each man would get his rest by sitting at the stern or on the bow of the boat. This relieved them from the oars.* The first few days were so hard on Julian's hands that they were bleeding where the blisters had broken and peeled off. He was so tired and sore he could not sleep.

---

*In the long route Julian traveled to reach the fur-trade region of the upper Missouri, he would have experienced several types of watercraft to transport men and goods. In the retelling of Julian's stories, Coryer made no distinction between the different vessels. In reality, from Montreal to Green Bay, Julian would have traveled in a *canot de maître* or Montreal canoe.

And he wished himself back home. If he could, he would have begged his father forgiveness and kissed his feet. If only he could have gone home. But it was impossible.

His homesickness would draw the older men's attention. But they showed him no sympathy. All they did was say, "Stick to it," and laugh. "You will harden up to it in time."

Well, he did, but it took about two weeks, and then he felt stronger and his longing for home gradually left him.

At last they arrived at Green Bay. The contents of the huge barge had to be transferred to smaller barges for the run up the Fox River, then down the Wisconsin River to its outlet into the Mississippi River.*

These barges were light. The framework was made of birch saplings and covered with buffalo hides cut square and sewed together with strong leather strings. Hot buffalo tallow was then poured into the seams. The inside and outside of the leather was also well oiled. The hair side of the leather was on the outside of the barge so as to protect it from snags or rocks. The hides were laid so as to protect itself by having the hair laying flat.**

Now the Long Trip Down the Rivers Begins

After the hard portage from the Fox to the Wisconsin River was finished, the boats were assembled in order, then the next lap of the trip began. This part of the trip was easier when labor was considered, but it was much more treacherous, for the river was shallow in places and sunken trees were fastened to the bottom of the river. The snags from the roots or limbs of the trees stuck up so as to tear holes in the bottom of the barges. When this happened the barges were brought aground and patches sewn over the torn holes.[18] Then hot tallow was poured over the patches.

The river was not the only danger. Many times they had to travel by night in order to steal past hostile Indians villages. During this part of the trip, two men were put on guard, relieving one another about every hour.

---

* At Green Bay, the men shifted the cargo to smaller canoes. The *canot du nord* was used on smaller streams and lakes.

** Albert is describing a bull boat. These boats were used only on the Missouri River and its tributaries.

A SHORT VISIT AT PRAIRIE DU CHIEN

The fur company had a trading post at Prairie du Chien, and it was necessary to stop here to deliver messages from Canada and pick up messages
from Prairie du Chien to deliver to St. Louis, which was the Hudson Bay
Fur Company main headquarters.* St. Louis was the place where large
ships were loaded to go to England, and where they unloaded ships of
trading articles such as beads, thread, calicoes, paints, alcohol, guns, rifles,
and ammunition, etc. The company got most of their furs and hides by
going up the Missouri River to the northwest.

This was Julian's first visit to Prairie du Chien. Though, at that time,
he had no way of knowing this village was later to become his final home.

At the time of his first visit, there were only a few fur traders living
along the riverbank and scattered about the [prairie]; the most settled
place was Frenchtown. The people living here then were about all French.
No one lived on the bluffs or near the bluffs. It was only a wilderness of
Indians and wild life.[19] The whites lived in fear of the Indians, [who] might
attack at any time.

As my grandfather left the mouth of the Wisconsin to turn northward,
the first white person he noticed on the riverbank was an old lady—or a
lady, rather. She wasn't very old at the time. She was Mrs. Cardinal. Her
husband was a fur trader. Her husband had died, and she was left alone in
their cabin, or log hut. She had many dogs to guard her, which caused my
grandfather to take notice of her and her place.[20]

Then they worked on up north, traveled on up north, to the fur trading posts, which were located along the riverbank [in the Main Village of
Prairie du Chien].** My grandfather said that at that time there were very
few people located in the city of Prairie du Chien. All there were, were
those few along the riverbank, the fur traders and a few other settlers,

---

* In 1829, only the American Fur Company had an office in Prairie du Chien. Joseph Rolette was the agent for American Fur and ran the Upper Mississippi Outfit of the Northern
Department. The headquarters of the Western Department of the American Fur Company
was located in St. Louis, Missouri. Within the Western Department was the Upper Missouri Outfit managed by Kenneth McKenzie and William Laidlaw. Among the fur traders
of the west, "The Company" always meant the American Fur Company.

** The Main Village of Prairie du Chien was located on an island west of the rest of Prairie
du Chien. Prairie du Chien was the name given to the entire prairie, not what the city is
today.

and then a few settlers along the east side of the slough, which forms an island between the river and the slough. It is part of Prairie du Chien.[21] Then from there, from the trading posts at Prairie du Chien, they went on down south to St. Louis.[22]

After the officers had communicated and everything was arranged, they were on their way to St. Louis.[23] Julian was toughened up to the hardships by now and was determined to make the best of it for the four years, which he had enlisted. The Mississippi River was not so treacherous. The water was deep and the current strong. This made it easier on the men at the oars.

Julian now began to take interest and enjoy this wild hazardous life as he grew stronger and more fit for it. On arriving at St. Louis, which was not such a large city at that time and Indians everywhere, Julian made up his mind to return to Canada when his four-year enlistment ended.

Now the Trip Up the Missouri Was About to Begin

This was the most strenuous trip rowing up against the strong current. The barges were loaded with merchandise to be traded for furs.[24] There were about five barges loaded with these goods.[25] A band of probably one hundred men manned the barges. It was a tedious, strenuous undertaking up against the swift Missouri current. At times, the current was so swift the men could barely keep them moving upward. No civilization at all along the Missouri.[26]

At last they reached the source of the Missouri River. Here was a fort. Everything was unloaded from barges and stored in the fort.[27] Then the barges were loaded with furs and hides, and then rowed down to St. Louis. Most of the men went back to St. Louis with them. A few men were kept up there to transfer this merchandise to another fort or forts in different parts of the northwest of the United States and Canada. Julian was one of them left to stay in the northwest.

Now this merchandise was loaded, after being arranged in large leather bags, on the ponies or western horses. A caravan [consisting of] forty horses and with two men was the way they arranged it.[28] Julian was held to help with the caravan of forty horses. Those horses were trained to follow one another single file. Each horse carried about two hundred pounds divided in packs of one hundred pounds on each side. [There was] a man on horseback to lead, and the other man at the rear to see that all horses kept going as they should.

There were always some of the horses that were not too well trained, and it was difficult to keep them trailing as they should. Some would try to get away.[29] Loading those two-hundred-pound packs on some of those broncos was also very strenuous and dangerous. Some of the horses would fight rather than to be loaded. But Julian took this all in fun and enjoyed the wild life as he grew stronger and able to do it.

This transferring things from one fort to another was done during the summer months. Winter was the time to collect furs [and hides] by trading with the Indians. It took weeks to make a trip with a caravan from one fort to another. And everything had to be unloaded from horses every evening so as to let horses rest and eat grass. During night, some of the horses had to be hobbled with strong leather straps to prevent straying away and so as to catch them in morning, and then reloading those two-hundred-pound packs was quite a task.

This [moving of caravans] was done across prairies which are now the Dakotas and Montana. Watering places for the horses were sometime far between, and the horses had to be without water for days. The men had water in leather bags on horse's back. Imagine how fresh this water was after being warmed by horse's body on one side and the sun on the other. But it was water anyhow.

The men's food on those trips was mostly dried buffalo meat. They dared not build fires for fear of Indians coming on them and killing them. There was plenty of game, but they dared not build fires to cook it. They were kept busy caring for the horses. Building fires on the prairies or even in the mountain valleys would cause the Indians to discover them.[30]

Some of the tribes of Indians were friendly and glad to trade with the Company whilst other tribes were hostile and dangerous. The whites had to be cautious how and where they traveled and lived.[31] Certain routes had to be followed so as to play safe, and also camping places had to be chosen so as to be safe from hostile Indians.

It took several days to make the trip [to an outlying post]. Then after resting and letting their horses rest, they would load their horses with hides and furs and return to the Missouri River.[32] Merchandise was transferred from eastern fort to western, and furs were transferred from western forts to eastern forts.

Now when winter came some of the men were kept busy cutting and hauling wood for fuel for the fort. The others were sent to collect furs from the Indians in the far northwest of United States and Canada. So far north, they used dogs to draw the sleighs laden with the merchandise to trade for furs all the way to the Indian settlements. On the way back, the sleighs were laden with furs, which they hauled back to the forts.[33]

Those trips meant much privation and hardships and danger for the men. They were always short on food. Buffalo meat was the only food they had then. They had to use snow to quench their thirst. They traveled until men and dogs were so tired they could not go any farther. The snow was deep so caves were shoveled in snowbanks, leaving a small hole to crawl in. Then buffalo hides were laid on ground to lie on, and another hide to cover [themselves], whilst dogs lay around on hides. This way all kept from freezing whilst resting.[34]

Julian's Adventure whilst Cutting Wood for the Fort

One winter Julian was sent with two other men to cut wood for the fort. Julian was the youngest of the three. The two other men were older than Julian and more able to accomplish the quantity of wood required or laid out for them to cut per day.[35] A certain amount of wood was expected to be cut by each man per day.[36]

Their rations comprised cornmeal, beans, and onions, and one load of ammunition given each man for a rifle or shotgun so they could get game for meat.

The older men sent Julian out to get the game because he was a better shot, and they were more able to cut wood.[37] They always had plenty of game meat. One day the Captain from the fort came to the log cabin they camped in. He found an oversupply of game, so he took it to the fort with him. So the men got wise to this and found a hollow tree not far from their hut and would hide their oversupply of game in that. Because the more time Julian spent hunting the harder the other two men had to work to cut the amount of wood set for them to cut. This wood was cut five miles from the fort. Some of the men were kept busy hauling the wood to the fort.

The workmen had to pay one dollar a pint for the salt they used, so they used it sparingly. The salt was kept on a shelf in the hut. The door in the hut was never locked, because they suspected no one to enter except the Captain or men hauling wood, and they knew none of them would steal the salt.

But the salt disappeared very fast. So the men suspicioned one another of using too much salt.[38]

THE SALT MYSTERY SOLVED

Julian was generally sent to do the cooking, so he had to take the blame of the salt disappearance.

One evening Julian entered the hut as usual to prepare supper, and to his surprise he found an Indian youth of about his own age. The Indian was by the salt with his hands filled with dried buffalo meat. As he ate, he would sink the meat in the salt and then bite off the salty part. This took the salt fast.

On seeing the Indian do this, Julian was angered very much, not so much as to the amount of salt that the Indian ate, but because it had caused hard feelings amongst the men. So Julian ordered the Indian out, accusing him of being a thief. As he stepped out of the door, Julian gave him a kick, which was not very harmful because Julian wore soft moccasins. This angered the Indian, and as he left, he turned and shook his fist at Julian and said, "I'll get you someday."[39] Time slipped by, and probably a month later, one evening after the men had eaten their evening meal, water was needed. There was not much in the birch bark bucket. So Julian decided to get some from the spring, which was not far from the hut, and there was a large tree near the door of the hut. As he stepped out, he noticed how bright the light of the moon was, so he looked up at the moon. On doing so, he noticed the form of a person crouched on a limb of the large tree near the door. On noticing this, he stepped back quickly and entered the hut. He grasped his rifle then stepped to the door. On taking a good look, he was convinced it was the young Indian whom he had found in the hut eating salt. The Indian had his bow and arrow ready to shoot Julian, as he would pass under the tree.

Julian could have shot the Indian with his rifle, but he did not want to kill. Therefore he spoke in Indian language and told the Indian that he could kill him. This he did not want to do, and if he promised him that he would never try to kill or harm him hereafter, he would not shoot him. The Indian promised this and jumped out of the tree and ran away and never bothered them anymore.

LIFE OF PRIVATION AND DANGER GETS ON THE MEN'S NERVES

Now, the men were paid only ten dollars per month. They had to pay one dollar per pint for salt to season their food, and they were compelled to cut a certain amount of wood per day and given a small amount of ammunition to kill game for their meat rations and a few onions and beans. The officers in the fort were living at ease with much better food and protected from danger.

The men got to thinking and speaking about it and how unfair this was. They decided they at least should get good food to eat. So they decided to go to the fort and have a conference with the officers concerning all this.

The officers at first objected and told the men to go back to work and be satisfied with what they were given.

The men got angry and told the officers, "We have been working to make it comfortable for you, and we have it coming, and we are going to have it. If you do not let us in the storeroom, we will break in regardless of your authority. We will get food or die."

The officers decided they had better open the storeroom door and did so. There was more than enough food and everything for all until spring, when they could go to St. Louis and get more.

This everything meant wheat flour, tea, sugar, and potatoes that had been grown near the fort.

Now this fur company that Julian worked for made much money because with an article valued at ten cents, they would probably get furs valued at one hundred dollars.[40]

Julian Decides to Go Back to Canada because He Is Disgusted with It All

But when the time came he had to change his mind. Let's see how it happened.

As I mentioned before, everything was transferred from the river fort to the western fort by caravans of horses manned by two men. Julian helped do this during the summer months. He had been working with the same man about all the time and had decided [his partner, who] was an older man at this job could be depended on and trusted.

Julian Faces Deceit and Robbery

As they were on their way westward, about three days travel from the fort and evening was coming, Julian's partner decided to camp not far from an Indian village. This was their general place for camping on other trips.

Julian noticed his partner acted rather strange and restless, but he imagined he was probably anxious to go and visit his Indian maiden, as he had been doing so on other trips.

When horses had been unloaded and hobbled to prevent them from straying away, they could eat their fill of grass then lie down and rest.[41] After they [the men] had eaten their evening meal, Julian's partner told him to lie down and rest, that he would be back soon as he was going to visit his friendly Indians. The Indians had been trading with the company and trusted the man and did not suspicion him any more than Julian did. But they were all to learn soon that they had been deceived.

A Sad Awakening for Julian

At daybreak, as usual, Julian awakened and arose and soon noticed his partner was not there. Julian felt that something was wrong, but what could have happened? He could not imagine. As he felt thirsty, he went to where they had put the leather water bags. The water was not there and could not be found. He then imagined his partner had gone for a fresh supply. So he decided to eat a bit of dried buffalo meat, which was also in a leather bag. The meat was also gone.

Julian became worried, and he went to count the horses. On doing so, he found that the two best horses were missing. This made it quite clear to Julian that his partner was gone.

Suddenly, Julian thought of his money, which he had saved for nearly four years. He had put his money in a special pocket and had sewn it in his buckskin trousers. He had slept in them, and he looked to be sure. As he expected, his pocket had been slashed with a knife, and his money was gone.

Julian felt so disgusted he sat down and wept bitterly. Then he consoled himself, looking at it as a punishment put upon him for having left his father in anger as he had.

JULIAN DECIDES TO MAKE THE BEST OF IT AND ENLIST FOR ANOTHER FOUR YEARS

He would be faithful to the company as long as he could. So he went to loading the two-hundred-pound packs of merchandise on the horses. This was hard to do alone, but it must be done. Some of the horses did not care to stand to be loaded. [With] no one to hold them, all he could do was to tie those to the gentle horses. He finally got the caravan of horses ready, but now he was alone to keep them following the trail.[42]

Just about when he was about to start, he heard the clattering of horses' hoofs on the hard prairie soil. On looking, he saw about two hundred Indians mounted and armed with bow and arrows coming directly towards him. He then knew more clearly what had happened to the partner, or rather what the partner had done.

The Indians stationed [themselves] about the company caravan. The chief rode up to Julian and asked him where his partner was? Julian quickly replied, "That is just what I would like to know." He told the chief that the two best horses were gone, also the bags containing the water and meat. Then he showed the chief where his pocket had been slashed and his money taken.

Then the chief said, "He did worse to us than he did to you." He said, "He stole the prettiest maiden of our tribe," and, he added, "He did worse to us because you can get back the same amount of money. But we can never get back the same maiden."

On finishing his speech, he gave the war whoop, calling his warriors together and advising them to go in different directions, and keep going until they found the man.

But the French-Canadian was too wise for the Indians. They never found [him], nor was he ever heard of again.

Julian Makes the Trip to the Fort Alone

Julian got his horses lined up, and, as the horses had been trained to follow the lead horse, they did very well. There was no food or water, and as Julian was afraid to leave his caravan alone and unprotected, he could not hunt for game. So he traveled two days and nights without food, just stopping his horses long enough to rest and eat a bit. At last he arrived at the river he had to cross, and glad to see it, he drank a little at a time until his thirst was quenched. The horses were unloaded by great effort and were led to the river for water. Then he hobbled them as usual.

Julian Is Now Very Weak and Decides to Try and Get Something to Eat—and He Gets It

Julian took his gun and started down the river[bank.] He had not gone far [when] he heard the honking of geese. He reached them and shot, killing two. Now, how could he get them from the river? He was too weak to swim, so he decided to make a crude raft of dry poles. Just then, he heard the chattering of Indians coming up the stream.

He let them come near enough so he could make them understand. He told them he had shot the geese and also told them of his long fast. They found the geese and put them in their canoes. The Indians then told Julian to come back with them, as they would set up camp where he had left his caravan.

At times he feared that the Indians would kill him and take the caravan. But he soon found out that they were a friendly tribe and meant well.

On arriving where his caravan was, the Indians landed and put up a tepee and spread a buffalo hide on the ground. They then told Julian to lie down on the buffalo hide in the tepee and rest. Julian then told them he must cook his geese, because he was about starved. The Indians laughed and said, "We will take care of your geese and get you something to eat; just lie down, and don't worry." So he decided to do as they told him and did so. They soon had a fire burning, and a [woman] soon brought him fish broth in a wooden spoon. It tasted so good he asked her to bring him more. She agreed and did, but only a spoonful at a time.

After doing so several times, she asked Julian if he was still very hungry. Julian told her he was not.

"Good," she said, and soon brought him a wooden bowl full of fish and broth and told him to eat his fill. She then told Julian that if she had fed him too much at first, it would have made him sick. When Julian had eaten his fill, the [woman] told him that he must lie down and rest. The men would care of the caravan and his horses. Julian obeyed with confidence. At daybreak, Julian awakened and got up to look for his caravan, but it was not to be found where he had left it.[43]

The Indians noticed him and came to him. [They] told him that all had disappeared during the night.

Julian answered, "Yes, but where has it gone to." The Indians laughed and told him that they had crossed everything across the river for him to be ready for him to be on his journey. They also gave him his two geese, well cooked and packed in a basket.

Julian was so well pleased with their kindness to him and asked them to accompany him across the river. They did so, and he gave each Indian a gift, regardless of what the company would think. An Indian also helped him with his caravan for one day. The Indian then returned to his tribe. On the second day, Julian reached the fort and told the officials what had happened. The company was well pleased with everything he had done, but did not offer to repay him the money that he had lost through the theft of his partner.

ANOTHER INCIDENT WHICH HAPPENED WHILST JULIAN WAS DRIVING THE CARAVAN

This happened on a trip from the river fort to the most western fort.

It was about sunset and by traveling any farther, it would have put them in the open prairie of a large valley in the mountains. They were in the shelter of a small hill covered with timber. It was a good place to camp, for they realized it would be risky to venture into the open prairie not know-ing whether there were Indians of an envious nature there to kill them.[44]

On stopping the caravan, the older man told Julian he would look around the valley to see if there were any Indians about. He would see them whilst Julian was setting up for camp. Julian kept an eye on his partner so as to be prepared for what might happen.

The partner rode a white horse, which was very fast and of great en-durance: one that could outrun the Indian ponies. But the Indians had spied him [first] and lay low in the tall grass. They let the white man get into their midst, then arose all around him. [They] caught his horse, and then grabbed him and pulled him off. Then [they] stripped the man of his clothing, then struck him and pricked him in the back with arrows. Then they let him go and shouted with joy on seeing him run away. But he ran in the opposite direction from where the caravan was, so if the Indians did try to trail him they would not find the caravan. When he was out of sight [of the Indians,] he circled back to where Julian was. Julian had seen all that had taken place to his partner, and he knew that his partner would not want to camp there. So he got everything ready for [them] to be on their way. When the man got back, Julian gave him part of his clothes, as they usually carried extra clothing in case of needing them.

They traveled all that night so as to get away from this tribe of Sioux. They stopped the next morning to let their horses eat and rest. During this time, Julian's partner told him that if possible he would get revenge on those Indians that had treated him so inhuman.

The following day, they arrived at the fort, and the grieved and angry man told the captain of what had happened, and that if ever he had a chance, he would kill those Indians. The captain told him not to do such a foolish thing, because by so doing it would cause a battle and no doubt the deaths of all the men in the fort. But the angry man would not listen or submit and swore revenge if he ever got the chance.

The Chance Comes and the Battle Takes Place

Two days later, whilst the men were preparing the hides and furs in packs for the caravan to take back to the river fort, the angered man shouted to the others, "Here comes the Indians that robbed and bruised me. Now I can get them." The captain told and forbid the angry man to shoot. They had the man's clothing tied to the saddle on the white horse's back.

The captain ordered his men to all get inside the barracks. The fort was built of logs split and set in the ground on end so that the thick part of the log would cover the thin parts of the other row. This made a thick wall of about ten feet out of the ground. The split sides were matched so as to form a wall the full thickness of the log. A strong door that could be bolted on the inside was the only opening to the fort wall.[45]

The Captain stood at the door and called to the Indians that headed the group. The Indian that led the white horse came to the fort door.

During this time, the angry man had got back into the barracks and gotten his rifle and got where he could shoot the Indian as he approached the fort door. He shot the Indian that led the white horse whilst the Indians were trying to apologize for what they had done. They realized that the horse and man belonged to the Company they were trading with and felt sorry for that which they had done. [They were] ready to make reparations for what they had done and be friendly in the future. The Captain would have forgiven them and saved the bloody battle. But anger had had its way.[46]

The killing of the one Indian angered the other Indians, and they would not listen to the Captain, for he would rather have turned the killer to them than risk them all being killed by the angered savages.[47]

THE BATTLE BEGINS

When the captain realized that there was no chance of reconciliation and that a battle was on, he hurriedly bolted the large door. The war whoop was heard. The leader ordered them to try and get over the barracks. One was to stand by the barracks and the others get on his shoulders and over the top.[48] The captain then told his men, "now we must fight or get killed by those savages." He told the men that he knew were the best and surest shots to get loaded rifles and stand watch at the top of the barricade. And sure enough the stronger Indians stood by the barricade, and the sure bow and arrow shots would stand on their shoulders. As they would show their heads over the top, the company sharpshooters would shoot them off. Those that could not shoot so well were kept loading rifles so that there was always loaded rifles.

The captain feared the Indians would set the barricade on fire, but they were not prepared to do it. When the Indians realized there was no use of trying any longer, because there was only part of their fighters there, they stopped. They left, all humming the war song of vengeance. This meant they would be back with reinforcements and no doubt prepared to set fire to the fort.

Now there was a tribe of friendly Indians camped not far from the fort, and the captain knew that they were not friends of the tribe that had attacked the company. So he sent the man who had killed the first Indian, telling this man to go to the tribe, which was on friendly terms with the company. He told him to take the white horse and ride as fast as possible. On arriving at the Indian camp, he was to ride three times around the camp and then stop and wait until the chief called him to come in. He was to tell the chief what the Sioux had done and say that the captain wanted him and his warriors to come to the fort.[49]

Now this messenger on horseback knew the Indians' rules, which was to first ride around the Indian camp thrice, then the chief would come out and beckon him in. This was done. The chief came out and beckoned the rider. He rode to the chief and delivered the message. The chief immediately called all his warriors and told them to prepare for a battle. This was soon accomplished. When they arrived at the fort, the captain told the chief that the other Indians had left humming the war chant. The captain also told the chief that the Sioux were tired, and he imagined they would have to stop to rest. Therefore, the friendly tribe did as the captain said.[50]

The chief told his warriors to track the defeated Indians and no doubt would find them resting and probably asleep. They did so and did it so cautiously they came on them, which were asleep in the open with no sentry. So the other tribe left their horses and sneaked up on them. They tomahawked them all in their sleep, then scalped them. They returned to the fort with the scalp sticking at the end of their bows to prove their victory, singing their victory chant.[51]

The captain was so glad that he invited them all in the fort. The men got busy, serving them tobacco and alcohol. They treated them to food and gave them alcohol to drink. At first the alcohol was diluted half water. When the Indians started to be intoxicated, he reduced the strength of the alcohol by adding more water and more water. The Indians spent the night drinking, and by morning they were sober. The Indians had a great time dancing, drinking, and smoking. The Captain then gave each one of the warriors a present and they left satisfied.[52]

When the Sioux chief would inquire at the fort as to what happened to his men, the captain would tell him that the men arrived safely at the fort and had left for their camp, and that was the last he had seen of them. In this way, he could avoid more trouble.

How Julian Was Frightened by a Dead Indian

By this time, Julian had traveled the northwest very much and was familiar to the Indian and his ways. He had learned to speak his language in the different dialects. Also he could endure this way of living with its hardships and privations of food, shelter, and drink.

[Therefore] he was chosen by the captain to go as a messenger to the different tribes that traded with the Hudson Bay Fur Company, to advise the Indians as to what kind of pelts were mostly in demand for the coming year, and how many they wanted.

This journey was very dangerous because some of the Indian tribes were unfriendly and would kill him if they got the chance. [Also], wolves, panthers, and mountain lions were always to be dreaded, especially when one traveled alone. So Julian had to be very cautious and sleep with one eye open and awaken at the slightest noise. He also had to live on what he could find or kill on the trip. He would travel until he was tired out, then rest.

One evening, as he was traveling through the forest, he spied a large tree, which he decided he would use as a shelter. So he started gathering leaves for a bed. It was getting dark, and as he lay down to rest, he looked upward into the treetop. To his surprise, he saw the form of a person stretched out on a large limb above him.

He was frightened, thinking it was a live Indian waiting for him to sleep, then come down and kill him. Julian leaped to shelter back of another tree. On taking a good look, he realized it was the body of a dead Indian. It had been tied to the high limb in the tree during the winter awaiting the ground to thaw for the burial, because the Indian had no tools [to] dig graves in the frozen ground.

When Julian was convinced it was a dead Indian, he returned to his pile of leaves to rest till daybreak. Julian said he could not help laughing, as he lay there, at his actions and fear of a harmless corpse.

How Did the Company Manage to Get the Number of Buffalo Hides They Wanted

The company knew of certain tribes of Indians that were dependable and would tell them how many buffalo hides they wanted. The Indians knew where the large herds of buffalo roamed. Then supposing if the company wanted one thousand hides, the chief would pick out fifty of his best riders and best shots with bow and arrows, mount them on fifty of his best horses or ponies, giving each man twenty arrows. The arrows they fastened to their shoulder in a leather pouch. Then they would locate a large herd. The fifty that were armed would go around about and hide in a draw amongst the sage brush, getting in a scattered position. The other Indians on horseback would round up the herd of buffaloes and get them running towards those that were hidden. When the Indians that were waiting saw them coming, they would lay flat to their horses' backs and wait until the buffaloes were all about them. They then started their horses running with the herd. This way the Indians were unnoticed by the buffalo and kept their horses with the herd so as not to be trampled by the buffalo. They would let their ponies run at their own pace. As they rode, they would sort out the buffalo with the best hide and would shoot the buffalo, aiming for the heart. Each arrow was supposed to kill a buffalo.[53]

When they had shot their twenty arrows, they would hold their ponies back and let the buffalo run past them. They dared not stop suddenly, because it would mean death to their ponies and themselves by being trampled. This way the herd would run past them and then they would ride back to where the buffaloes were that they had shot. Then the whole tribe would get busy skinning the animals. After the skinning, the hides were stretched out on the ground to dry. When dry enough, they were rolled into packs and loaded on the ponies' backs to be carried to the fort. Those hides, by trading articles to the Indians, would cost [the company] about one dollar per hide.

The carcasses were mostly all left to the wolves. The Indians would cut out the choice parts, slice it, and dry it. The tallow was saved for various purposes.

How Traders Managed to Get Much for Their Merchandise

The Indians were anxious to get rifles and would pay most anything for them. And to get much for the rifles, the company deceived the Indians. For instance, in order to make the Indian believe the rifles would shoot really farther than they really could, they would do this.

The Indians camped on a certain curve on the river, and the traders knew where the camp was. There was another bend in the river a mile away. The traders would pick out two large trees that could be seen from where the Indians were camped. The men would get at close range and shoot a bullet in each tree, and then they would go to the Indians' village. [The men would] show them the rifles and tell them that they could shoot a bullet in each big tree at the bend of the river a mile away. The Indians would doubt them, so the traders would shoot at the trees, then tell the Indians to see if the shots hit. Some of the Indians would go and, with knives, dig out the bullets to show the chief. Then the chief would give the traders any amount of furs for the rifles.

Another Trick to Get the Hides for Guns

After a fresh snow, a trader would go towards a nearby Indian camp. As deer were very plentiful, he would spy a deer and shoot it. He would note from what direction the animal had come, and then he would go to the Indians. [He would] tell them he had a rifle that would kill by shooting on the track in the snow.

To prove this, he would go in the direction of where he had shot the deer and find the track in the snow. [He would] say, "I think I can get this deer, the track is fresh." He would point his rifle the way the track went, then shoot down the track. He then would send the Indians to see if they could find the animal. Of course, they would find [the deer] freshly killed. That would prove that the gun would kill by shooting on the track.[54]

The Indians were easily deceived at first, but they soon learned of the traders' tricks. They then began to get angry and rebellious, and it caused them to hate the whites. As a result, there were many bloody skirmishes between the red man and the whites.

JULIAN MAKES UP HIS MIND TO GO HOME IN CANADA FOR THE SECOND TIME

Julian had served about his second term of enlistment of four years, which all told made eight years of this treacherous life. He had saved about all of his money, so that he could go home in a respectful way.

The company was on their way down the Missouri River to St. Louis.[55] He traveled the Missouri River and had almost reached St. Louis, when he began to feel ill. He had a high temperature. On reaching St. Louis, he was taken to the company log building called their hospital. A man was left to care for him. This man had taken a course in medicine and was called a doctor. On taking Julian's case in consideration, he determined that Julian was affected with typhoid fever. Julian was very sick and for weeks wavered between life and death.

During the long eight years of service in the company, Julian had not missed one day of service due to sickness. Now, on the last days of his enlistment before quitting this way of life to return to his old home in Canada to his relatives and friends, he was stopped by this terrible sickness which lasted long enough to drain him of most of his four long years of his savings. He had planned in using this money to get home and have enough left to appear and live respectfully enough to get other employment.[56]

Julian realized he had been punished for his misbehavior the second time. Julian's savings had first been taken by a thief and by sickness the second time. He then said, "God has punished me for my revengeful act towards my father."

JULIAN DECIDES TO MAKE UNITED STATES HIS HOME

[Julian] finally got strong enough to care for himself. He had a little money left, and with this he bought forty acres of land then adjoining the village of St. Louis. He built a log hut on it and was about to start farming when the Black Hawk War was declared, and Uncle Sam called young men to enlist and take up arms against the Indians.

Julian again picked up courage and enlisted in the army to fight Black Hawk. This he did until the war ended, and he was honorably discharged.*

JULIAN SEES WHITE SOLDIER SKINNED ALIVE BY INDIANS

As Julian traveled northward with his company to where Black Hawk was to be found and captured, they had to pass by other tribes of peaceful Indians. The captain of this cavalry commanded his men not to fire a gun unless so ordered by him. But there were some of the soldiers that felt so revengeful towards all Indians, regardless of what tribe they belonged to.

As they were passing by this Indian camp, one of the revengeful soldiers noticed an old Indian woman sitting on a log combing her hair. This bloodthirsty soldier said, "Here is a good target. I will try it." The others near him tried to prevent him from shooting. But he raised his rifle and shot and killed the woman instantly. This angered the Indians, and in no time the whites were surrounded by warriors with bow and arrows, rifles, and lances. The Indians outnumbered the whites ten to one. The captain ordered his men to halt. On finding the guilty man, he told the chief that this man had disobeyed him. [He told the Indian leader] that he could do whatever he chose to do with him. But not to molest any of the other men.

This was satisfactory to the chief. [He] ordered his men to make four stakes and get four strong strings. This they did. He had the guilty man stripped of his clothing and laid him on his back on the ground. They drove a stake by each hand and foot, which they tied securely with the leather strings.

When he was fastened to the stakes, the chief ordered four of his men to start skinning him, a man at each hand and foot. The man lived long enough to have half of his skin removed, and then he died. The soldiers were made to stand around and see their comrade soldier die to satisfy their revenge.

---

*Albert may have shared events in Julian's life out of order. Julian's service in the Black Hawk War would have been during his employment with the American Fur Company or between working for American Fur and Pratte, Chouteau and Company.

When Julian Was Discharged He Returned to St. Louis

Yes, Julian returned to St. Louis, expecting to see his log hut awaiting him. But during his absence, the hut had been burned to ashes. This changed his plans, so he decided to work about St. Louis and let his forty [acres] of land. The land he then owned is now covered with part of the City of St. Louis.

The first job Julian got was to oversee slaves. He expected that he would have to just tell the slaves what to do and see that they did it. But when the slave owner presented him with a long rawhide whip, Julian asked him what he was supposed to do with the whip. The slave owner told him, "You are to drive twenty Negroes that are to pull a plow. You hold the plow and when a man lags back, slash him with the whip."

Julian handed the whip back and quit the job on the spot.

After Julian turned down the job [of driving slaves], he got a job painting. He did this well because he had learned how to paint with his father back in Canada. While working in St. Louis, he met the young lady which later became his bride and wife.

Her name was Lucretia Lessard. The Lessard family had also come from Canada, but from another village or parish, "La Riviere du Loup," the French for "Wolf River."

[The Lessards] had moved from Canada with several other families to New Orleans, Louisiana. Whilst living there, the family had suffered the loss of the father and one son, named Charles. Contagious diseases raged, such as cholera, yellow fever, and smallpox of the worst form. The whole family had smallpox, which took the father and son.

This disheartened the mother of the family, so she decided to move back northward. She still had three sons and two daughters. The eldest daughter, Lucretia, married Julian.[57] The other daughter married Frank Gokey.[58] The marriages took place in the first old cathedral in St. Louis. The Lessards moved from New Orleans to Baton Rouge, Louisiana. They lived there awhile. There, the water was very impure and had to be boiled to be fit to drink. This caused them to move to St. Louis. After Julian's marriage, the dreaded cholera disease hit St. Louis. God spared Julian and the Lessard family.[59]

Doctors claimed that the disease was brought on by eating certain food. No doubt this was why some families were spared. The doctors forbid people the eating of fresh fruits, cucumbers, muskmelon, green corn, and also fresh meats. The disease was so bad and people died so fast that proper care of the dead was forbidden by the board of health. Proper burials to the dead could not be given them. They died so fast, the board of health ordered men to dig trenches in cemeteries. [They] had drays, which were drawn by mules, to keep traveling the streets, one man driving and two men on each side of the street. The men had the authority to enter all buildings. On finding a dead body, [they] would roll the dead in sheets or a blanket it was laying on and carry it to the dray. The men would load the bodies crosswise of the dray as they moved along the streets.[60]

They did not wait until told of a death, but entered all houses. When a dead or apparently dead body was found, they took it away regardless of what anyone said. This was ordered by [the] board of health. The bodies were hauled to the cemeteries so fast they had to lay some two deep in the trenches. Then other men covered the bodies with dirt as soon as possible. This was done to prevent disease from spreading.

JULIAN IS DISGUSTED WITH THE SOUTH AND MOVES NORTHWARD

Julian moved from St. Louis to Dubuque. He found work at his trade painting. It was mostly indoors decorating. Being accustomed to the outdoor life, painting got the best of his health. On learning that a man and wife were wanted near Galena at the mines where they mined and melted lead and zinc, he decided to try that. Julian worked at the smelter, and his wife did the cooking at the camp. The men worked day and night in shifts, but it was hardest for Lucretia, for she had to have a meal at noon, six p.m., midnight, and six a.m. She stood it for a while, but it was too much for her. And the melting of lead and zinc was also injurious to Julian's health.

By melting the lead and zinc mineral, arsenic poison is formed and escapes in dust form. So much of it accumulated about the place that it killed all vegetation for rods distance around. So much formed about the melting pots and on the floor, it was collected and wheeled out in wheelbarrows and dumped in a pile away from the place. It was so rank and poisonous that a snake thrown in the pile alive would squirm a few times, immediately bloat, and burst from the effects of poison.

Lucretia had to keep fresh milk handy because occasionally a man would come in feeling the effect of the poison and fresh milk was the only thing that would counteract the poison and save their life. One man resisted too long and died from the effects of the arsenic.

JULIAN MAKES UP HIS MIND TO GO FARMING

[Julian] was persuaded by his two brothers-in-law, Frank and John Lessard, to come to Prairie du Chien.[61] The [Lessard] boys had remained in St. Louis whilst Julian lived in Dubuque. They had been working for a ranchman out of St. Louis to catch, tame, and train the wild western horses. When he would have about two hundred trained to lead and accept the saddle so he could sell them, he would come northward. [He would] stop in every locality where he expected they would need horses. These horses were also trained to ford the rivers, the Mississippi included.[62]

This way the Lessard boys got to Prairie du Chien. They were so taken up by the surrounding country, and especially by the pure spring water. They refused to return to St. Louis with the ranchman. They settled here and took to farming. Wheat was about the only moneymaking crop. All of this induced Julian to go to farming.

As to the Lessards, who were still young and single.[63] On hearing of the 1849 opportunities of making money in California in the gold rush of forty-nine, they gave up their land claims. In company of three other Prairie young men, which were Cosmos and Oliver Cherrier and a Mr. Rossou [Rousseau], they went to California by the company of a large caravan of prairie schooners or covered wagons, westward across prairies and through mountains on the Oregon Trail.[64]

At evening, [they] came to a halt and would place their covered wagons or "prairie schooners" in a circle, so as to make a fortification against a possible attack by hostile Indians. They would set up tents and keep their oxen or horses, and people, inside the circle of wagons. Each man stood on guard in turn all night to make sure the Indians did not get them.[65]

When they arrived at Death Valley, they needed water very much.[66] On noticing a spring of water, apparently clear, they drove to it with intentions of having a good drink for themselves and animals. But they were stopped by a man put there by the United States government officials to warn people and prevent animals from drinking this water. It was rank poison. To convince them, he showed them the many skeletons of men and animals that had died by drinking the water from this spring. Those skeletons were the remains of once thirsty humans and animals, which drank of this poison water. The watchman advised them where to go to find pure water, not so far away.[67]

The caravan finally reached its destination. Some went one way, others took another direction, all seeking their fortunes. The five men named above kept together, and when they learned that labor was badly needed, they first engaged in the building of barns, which were used for storing away wheat and other grain to keep it dry during the rainy season, so that it could be threshed out by flail by hand.

The five men from Prairie du Chien built several barns for the Franciscan monks. They worked hard and put in long days. Because they built those barns by contract, by so doing they cleared ten dollars per day per man.

While working for the monks, they were restricted to the monks' orders and rules. This meant arise at a certain time, go to Mass, then breakfast, and then to work. Before lunch they went to the mission to pray. This was the rule both morning and afternoon, and always to bed at a certain hour. The men all agreed that this kind of life kept them in shape, so they improved in health and work. When finished here they went to work.[68] They were paid one dollar per hour. This was very strenuous work. They managed to stand it, except Cosmos Cherrier, who was not so strong.

The boys finally imagined they had made their fortunes and decided to return to Prairie, which they did by taking a ship around by way of Cape Horn to New Orleans, and then by [steamboat] to Prairie du Chien.

On arriving home, Mrs. Lessard asked her son John if he had made his fortune. He answered, "I have enough gold coins to fill one of your stockings." The mother doubtfully got him one of her stockings. John filled to the brim with gold. The four others had about the same.

Now Back to Julian

Julian settled on a forty-acre tract of land at the top of Limery Coulee. He was the first white man to settle on this ridge. He soon had a good yoke of oxen broken and well trained.

A man that then owned and lived on the now Swingle farm, wanted to trade Julian his farm for his yoke of oxen to go to California with the caravan in the 1849 gold rush.[69] Julian desired to follow the caravan to California. But his wife objected. She said, "We have traveled enough. Here we have the best of water, and on those bluffs we can grow most everything necessary for a living, and here on the bluffs we have no ague or malaria. I say we stay here." At that time those living in the valley got their water from dug wells curbed with rock. Those wells were dug to below the river level, and water was drawn up with a windlass, a chain, and an oaken bucket. The water in those wells sometimes got quite stale.

The ague [malaria] is now a thing of the past, but then nearly everyone living in the valley would get this fever and ague during summer. Quinine and whisky was about the only remedy to prevent or stop this when one got it.

The ailment got on its rampage early in summer. It would generally start on a person in the forenoon from nine to eleven o'clock. It started with a chill, and the chill kept getting worse until one would be so cold. No matter how much covers one used or what they drank or how hot the weather was, the person would shake with cold for about one hour, then the chill would leave and the person would be burning with fever, and such a headache. This lasted for about three hours. The person was left weak and sick for the remainder of that day. People would get this every other day, and if it started on one at nine it would come on at the same hour every other day.

When Julian had his forty-acre farm about under cultivation, his other brother-in-law Joseph Lessard who was married to Monica Limery, daughter of John Limery, ... lived on the old Indian trail in Frenchtown opposite the Limery Coulee and owned the Limery Coulee.[70]

Joseph Lessard realized it was best for him to get on a tract of land and go farming, as he had four children. So Julian told him he could have the forty he was living on, and he would locate on another forty about one-half mile west.[71]

This forty also had a wonderful spring on it. So, he did so to help out his brother-in-law. It was easier for Julian to start on a wild forty because he had only one child, Joseph, which was born September 19th, 1845. Julian also had good oxen to work with which meant much. [He] soon broke up the land for wheat farming.[72]

The buildings were all built of logs chinked with strips of wood, then plastered with mortar made of yellow clay in and out. The house was whitewashed with lime inside. Two coats would make the wall white.

Some huts were built with two wide doors at each end wide enough to drive in with a yoke of oxen pulling a log in opposite the fireplace. The log was then cut up in cuts about three feet long and rolled in the fireplace. This would last for a few days.

They had no screen for doors or windows, and in the summer mosquitoes and flies welcomed themselves in. Occasionally a friendly snake could be seen hanging over the window frame, so as to be able to sleep. They made smoke with rotten wood. This they called a smudge to keep the mosquitoes away. The mosquito was very plentiful but not so many flies. There were not so many flies those days because there was not the filth here to cause the fly to live by.[73]

ASPECTS OF LIFE ON THE CORYER FARM

Now one would wonder why people settled on the bluffs where it was hilly and farther away from the river. Well, the reason was not because the land was cheaper, because they could have entered land on the prairie for the same price, $1.25 per acre. But they wanted to be where they could have the pure spring water instead of water from dug well drawn up with chain and oaken bucket, then put into another wooden bucket. There was no such thing as a tin or metal pail; it was either wood or earthen crockery.

And another reason of living on the bluffs was to get away from the mosquitoes, which were a pest in the valley. And another reason was to get away from malaria and fever and ague, which nearly everyone got....

Quinine and whisky mixed by druggist[s] was taken to stop it. This ailment disappeared just about when gasoline motors of different kind[s] came in existence. As we all know the exhaust from the motors throw off poisonous gasses which fall to the ground and also oil dropping on the ground, and then when a heavy rain falls it washes this down into the river and spreads on the stagnant ponds where the ague and malaria germs forms and mosquitoes carry them from [people] to people.

Wheat was about the only moneymaking crop; there was always a ready sale for it. Therefore much wheat was raised about Prairie du Chien. Forty bushels per acre was the average crop at the time.

The climate at that time was favorable for wheat and oats growing. But the only corn that would mature here was the hard, round-kerneled Yankee corn, a ninety-day corn. It was as hard as popcorn, short kernel and only five or six rows of kernels to the cob but long cobs.

The temperature changed; the summers got longer, and the nights stayed warmer, and gradually the dent corn could be grown and ripen here, and as this happened the grain crops were smaller.

But a flour mill was built on the riverbank opposite the southwest corner of the Villa Louis property. This mill ground all the wheat that was raised for miles around as far as could be hauled with oxen and horses also from Iowa. [The farmers] hauled it across the Mississippi River in winter on the ice. The flour was taken south by steamboats and sold for consumption in the south.

Julian raised and trained three yoke of oxen. He used them to break land. [To do] that, it is [necessary] to pull a plow that turned a twenty-inch furrow. The power of three yoke of oxen was not necessary to turn the soil over, but there were much underbrush small saplings with hickory taproots as large as four inches. The oxen would straddle the saplings and bend them over. This helped the plow to cut the roots. When Julian's son Joseph reached the age of fourteen years, he learned to drive three yoke of oxen. It was done by commands and with a whip.

No lines or bridles were used on oxen and no harness either, just a yoke and a chain fastened to [the] plow. The oxen were trained to come side by side and the driver would place the yoke on their necks, then put the U-shaped stick up through the yoke. The commands were "get up" to go forward, "whoa" to stop, "back" to back, "gee" to turn to right, and "haw" to turn to left. The whip was to be used if commanded to "get up" and no response; a lash on the sides. If commanded to stop or back they did not stop, they got the whip on the nose.

Oxen were not subject to try to run away; they were generally too lazy. But most of them if given their time would pull with terrific power. Now after this land was broken or plowed the work began shaking all those roots out and piling them to burn.

Julian and son broke the first furrows on Limery ridge and also Famechon ridge for Famechon and LeClare. They were both wealthy men and hired this work done. [Julian broke land] also for the Sebastians when they located in the Campbell coulee.

Julian Gets a Land Grant of 160 Acres from the U.S. for Having Served and Having Been Honorably Discharged from the "Black Hawk War"

After being well started farming at Prairie du Chien, Julian got a notice that he was entitled to a 160-acre land grant in Nebraska about where Omaha now is.

At the time, this was a wilderness and Indians were hostile with the whites as they traveled in prairie schooner caravans westward to the west coast. The government planned [that] by giving each Black Hawk War veteran a land grant of 160 acres there, they would take care of the Indians because they were accustomed to fighting Indians.

Julian was anxious to go because he enjoyed this wild life, and he knew that this land was good farmland. He had been there several times whilst working for the Hudson Bay Fur Company. But his wife refused to go. When he insisted, she told him to go, and her and her son Joseph would stay here.

Now Judge Bronson [Brunson] heard of this, so he offered Julian enough money to buy 160 acres adjoining his forty he was located on and owned.[74] So Julian sold his rights to Judge Bronson and bought 160 acres, which made him a tract of 200 acres in the town of Prairie du Chien. Mr. Bronson was a government surveyor and knew this land in Nebraska to be good and in time worth much.

About the year 1853 the deer were very plentiful here. Droves of as many as twenty were seen in the hills. About that year there came a fall of about twelve inches of snow in December, and after the snow a sleet which formed a sheet of about one-fourth inch of ice. Then about the latter part of December another such a snow[storm] and crust of ice. Then the early part of January, another fall of snow and a crust of ice. There was about three feet altogether of this.

Now the deer sometimes would slip and fall on steep side hills and would get to sliding fast and hit something which killed them. Others would break through the crust and [in] [struggling] to get out would cut their legs so that they would die. Thereby most of the deer died during this winter. Some men made well by going in the woods and skinning the dead deer and selling the hides. Most of the quail died during this winter by being covered by snow.

[In about 1850] Julian went to Canada to visit his father, who was very old at the time. But Julian wanted to ask his father's forgiveness for having left home in anger. Money was scarce, but Julian gave his father fifty dollars in gold. Thereby Julian told the Valleys and Prew[s] [Vallee and Proulx families] of the new country here and the milder climate, so they all came to Prairie shortly after.[75] There was also two older sons of the centurian [Antoine Valley], which were Olezim [Olizeme] and Oliver.[76] Olezim located at Harpers Ferry [Iowa] after marrying a Miss Marcus.

JULIAN'S LAST DAYS

Julian was charitable to all. If anyone stopped at his place, he was welcome to what he had. Indian or white, it made no difference. They need not leave his place hungry or cold or tired, and it seems that God helped him to get those things to help others with. His health was good up to the October before he died. He was clearing land as he usually did in the month of October. He felt thirsty and was quite warm from the exertion. So he went to a spring nearby [and] took a good drink of cold water. [He] then sat on a rock to rest a bit. Suddenly he felt chilly. This got him to go back to work to kill the chill, but he could not get warm so he went home. His wife wrapped him in warm blankets and gave him warm drinks, [and] finally stopped the chill. But from that time on he got worse until it turned to dropsy, which caused his death on January 7, 1881, at the age of sixty-seven years.*

---

*Dropsy is an old term for the swelling of soft tissues due to the accumulation of excess water. Today one would be more descriptive and specify the cause, such as congestive heart failure.

PART 4

BEYOND THE NATURAL WORLD

I n her interview with Albert Coryer, Florence Bittner asked Albert to "tell us a little something of the faith cure of the early French-Canadians." She must have been curious about a part of the French culture of Prairie du Chien that was known but little discussed with non-French residents.

Charming, *charme* in French, is the saying of words or prayers, used outside the context of a church, for healing purposes. Charming has been practiced in France since the early days of the Catholic Church. Different charms are used depending on the ailment. The gift of charming came to the New World with the French, and folklorists have documented its continued practice in Quebec and Louisiana.[1]

Those who lived within the French community of Prairie du Chien in the nineteenth and twentieth centuries knew the identity of these charmers, who included two of Albert's relatives within the Lessard family. But this knowledge remained within the Prairie du Chien French community and was seldom spoken about among community members. Respected charmers were modest and unassuming about their gift. Healers could not offer their services; they could only respond to specific requests. A patient could put money on a table or bed so that the healer could pick it up, but direct payment was not acceptable, and even saying "thank you" was believed to break the power of the charm. Each charmer claimed various strengths, with the ability to heal only certain problems. Those who possessed or benefited from the ability believed that there was a part of the natural world that could not be explained. Healing through laying hands on the body or quietly reciting words and prayers cannot be explained by physical science, but many residents of Prairie du Chien believed in the practice. Of the known charmers among Albert's contemporaries, almost all were of French-Canadian heritage.

As a faith healer himself, Albert Coryer knew that more than natural ability was needed for charming. A faith healer needed to know the charm formulae and prayers themselves, and the knowledge's source was crucial. The healing gift had to be handed down within the community. As Albert told Mrs. Bittner, he learned from Charles Valley, who had learned from

Albert, pictured in front of his home on North Beaumont Road at age eighty-two, considered himself a faith healer. DONNA A. HIGGINS

Basil Gagnier, who had been instructed by early Canadian settler Jean Baptiste L'Emerie (whom Albert refers to as "Mr. Limery"). Albert therefore was part of the third generation of charmers in Prairie du Chien and would teach others. Though Albert shared this information with Mrs. Bittner, he never mentioned his gift in all the stories he recorded himself.

But his gift was common knowledge in Prairie du Chien at the time, and people who lived in the north half of town sought him out for this purpose. Like the other charmers, Albert took his gift seriously and expected others to do so as well. As he once told a young man who asked for his help, a person must believe in the power for healing to occur, and "it won't work if you are not serious."[2] As the charmers did not promote

their ability, the record of their cures has disappeared with the passing of
the patients. Thanks to Albert and Mrs. Bittner, the story of Basil Gagnier
has been preserved.

Perhaps because of his ability, Albert demonstrated a fascination with
the unexplainable or supernatural. He recounted the "will-o-the-wisp"
story included in part 1, and he fully believed in the power of prayer to
drive the passenger pigeons from the land and their eventual return after
ninety-nine years. In addition to these stories and his account of the faith
cure, Albert shared three other stories of supernatural phenomena, having
to do with family members or others who had passed. Connection to family was a key in the practice of charming. In saying the charm or prayer, a
charmer would recite not only the name of the patient but also the names
of the charmer's parents and grandparents, drawing on the power of family connections to strengthen the charm. Some at the time believed these
bonds extended into the afterlife. Members of Albert's family had claimed
to receive messages from people who had died. As with all his stories, Albert had learned of these special occurrences from his grandparents. But
Albert would share these phenomena only with his own family members.
At a time when Christian beliefs did not accommodate giving credence
to "ghosts" or communication from the afterlife, perhaps Albert felt the
need to be careful with whom he shared these particular stories. And so
he wrote down what he called "Ghost Stories," intended only for his niece,
nephew, and cousins.

Charmers had a way with words, words that healed. Albert obviously
had a way with words, not only in healing but in storytelling.

Coryer's Ghost Stories and a Conversation about Faith Cures

MRS. BITTNER: Mr. Coryer, the French had what they called a faith cure, which we've heard a great deal about, and I don't believe there is too much told of that in the early histories of the French, I wonder if you could tell us a little something of the faith cure of the early French Canadians.

MR. CORYER: Yes, it was brought here . . . with . . . the first settlers. Mr. Limery was the man that first did this, and knew this cure, and then it was handed down to others. Each one, whoever knew this faith cure, could hand it down to three others before his death. And Mr. Limery handed it down to Mr. Basil Gagnier, and then Mr. Gagnier handed it down to others and so on, and there are still some in Prairie du Chien that know this and . . . make use of this faith cure. It don't only cure rattlesnake bites, but . . . several other ailments also.

And to prove that it can cure rattlesnake bite—my grandmother [Langford] was bitten by a rattlesnake when they first settled up on Shanghai Ridge near in the Town of Eastman. One evening an old . . . bookseller, an agent, . . . drove in the yard with an old white horse, and the horse was tired, and the man was old and tired also, and asked if he could stay there overnight with them. And . . . my grandmother, of course, told him that if he wanted to put up with what they had there, that he was welcome. And so he said he would put up with anything just so he could have a place to rest for him and his horse, and something to feed his horse, and to eat.

And my grandmother told him that her husband, my grandfather Langford, had run out of old hay, that if he wanted hay to feed his horse he'd have to take the scythe and mow his horse some hay, because her husband had come in tired and wouldn't feel like mowing too much hay. [So] he says, "If I had the scythe, if you'll give me the scythe, I'll surely do that and I'll also mow some for your husband's oxen, also." And so my grandmother knew where the scythe was, . . . hanging in an oak tree not far from the house.

And so she went to the tree, and she stepped near the tree to take the scythe down. There was a large rattlesnake there, and she touched the snake with her foot, and the snake bit her on the ankle. And of course she brought the scythe to the old man, and at the same time she says, "I've been bitten by a rattlesnake. There was a snake at the foot of the tree and he bit me on the ankle." The old man was very much excited and he realized what it meant, and so he says, "Have you a shovel or spade here?" he says. "I'll dig a hole near the porch and you just put your foot and, and leg down in there, up to your knee, and then," he says, "cover it up with the wet clay and that will draw the poison out." And so my grandmother got him the shovel, and he did that, and she sit on the porch and buried her ankle and leg and foot in the clay, and my grandfather came in from work in the field, and there he saw her sitting there in that condition, so he quickly asked her what happened.

She told him, and he put his oxen away as quick as he could and went to the neighbors to see if he couldn't get other help, told the womenfolks about it, and in no time there was a crowd there, and they were all trying to do all they could. Some said, "Give her whiskey, all she can drink." And my grandmother had never drank any alcoholic drinks at all, wasn't accustomed to that, but still during the night she drank nearly a quart of whiskey, and it didn't seem to take any effect. There was so much poison in her system from the snake, the whiskey didn't seem to take any effect on her at all. And some said, "Take chickens and just cut their heads off and split them open and bandage . . . the ankle with those chickens, put the warm chickens on there, and it will draw the poison out." Which it did to a certain extent. My grandfather said that he threw those chickens—he used twelve of them during the night—and he took those chickens and dumped them in a hollow stump not very far from the house—and he said by morning this stump was just flowing over with a white foam from the poison from those chickens, which he burned afterwards, of course.

And then by morning, about daylight, my grandfather's house wasn't far from the road, that led well from Prairie du Chien up by East Linden and then down to what they called Citron Valley, and there was some of their relatives, these people that were traveling, going from Frenchtown to Citron Valley to visit their relatives there. And they noticed the crowd, and that was the old-fashioned way, if they'd notice anything like that they wondered if they couldn't help. So they stopped in and asked what had happened and if they . . . couldn't help. And so they were told about my grandmother being bitten by a rattlesnake, and they did all they could all night, and she was getting worse. The swelling was nearly up to her body and also her leg was also spotted, the color of a rattlesnake. And so my grandfather listened to them and . . . those French people told my grandfather that if he'd go down to Mr. Basil Gagnier and tell him about it and ask him to come up . . . with this faith cure, using this faith cure, that he'd cure my grandmother.

And so my grandfather quickly picked a boy out of the crowd that had . . . just a small horse, a saddle horse, and so he told the boy to learn from those people where to go to get Mr. Gagnier, and which the boy did. Some of them giggled and laughed about this, thinking that this just being a faith cure that would cure this. And my grandfather says, "Now this is no time to laugh. My wife is about dead and we have tried all we could all night, and we want to be sincere about this and try it as, as we should." So the boy went down for Mr. Gagnier on horseback, and . . . my grandfather told him not to save the horse, to travel right along fast and get there as quick as he could, which the boy did, most too much, drove the poor horse too fast, and when he got there the horse was very warm, white with lather from running.

So Mr. Gagnier just happened to be driving in his yard as the boy come. He had been to Mass. He had [driven] down to Mass with a . . . horse and a cart, and the boy told him what had happened, that he was wanted up at Langford's. And when the boy had told him where [the] Langfords lived, where he should go, the boy says, "Take the pony and get on his back and ride back as quick as you can." He says, "Your horse is about dead now. You've driven him too fast. You take care of your horse, brush him down, and give him little bits of water now and then, and cool him off slow, and then start back home slow with him if you want to save your horse. I'll drive my own horse."

So he jogged on up there and got up to Langfords'. And when he got there, my grandfather brought him in, and he told the ladies that were in there to cut just a slit in my grandmother's nightgown so that they could put a string around her leg near her body and then have the ends extend out through this slit in her nightdress so that he could tie them in certain knots that he made and at the same time saying prayers that he should say. Which he did, and then he told my grandfather, he said, "Now your wife, in about three days, will be getting up and walking around the house, and when she does that, naturally... the swelling will be going down, and the string will drop. Now, tell her not to bother with the string, to just go about her work, never mind the string, and when she loses it, not to look for it. Just don't bother about the string."

But my grandfather... told my grandmother about this, but she'd forgotten, or feared that the swelling would go up again. When she did get about the house, the string fell down to her ankles, so she quick grabbed the string and pulled it back way up where it was at first. And the swelling followed right up to the string. And she told my grandfather this, and "Well," he says, "The man told you not to bother with the string. Let the string go wherever it would." And well, the next time it dropped, which it did, and she left it go and lost the string. [She] never found the string. But anyway, in a few days, a week or so in all, she was perfectly well. The swelling had gone down; her leg didn't hurt her anymore, and she was well. She was never bothered with that anymore. He had cured her.

And then Mr. Gagnier asked my grandfather to see this place where this snake was when he bit my grandmother. So my grandfather took Mr. Gagnier out there where the snake... was coiled when he bit my grandmother by the tree. And before this, ... in the morning as soon as daylight came, the boys of the neighborhood took dogs and they wanted to find this snake. They hunted with dogs and clubs, but they never could find the snake. But anyway, Mr. Gagnier told my grandfather he could go back to the house now. And the boys, of course, were curious and they watched him. There was a rail fence near the place so Mr. Gagnier fixed himself a switch out of hazel brush and set on the rail fence. It wasn't long that he got off of the fence, walked to the spot where the snake was, and started switching and talking French, saying something in French, and switching down at the ground. The boys all [ran] there and there was a big rattlesnake sneaking away as fast as he could go, crawling away. And the boys said, "Wait, wait, we'll kill him. We'll fix him."

And Mr. Gagnier said, "Never mind, I'll take care of that snake. He'll never bother anybody anymore. He'll never bite anyone. I'll take care of him. You go back," So the boys went back, and of course, Mr. Gagnier took his time, and got in his cart and drove away, and as soon as he'd gone out of sight, the boys took their clubs and dogs, and they were going to find that snake and kill it. They hunted the best they could and had the dogs hunt also, but they never found the snake. And of course, my grandmother got well and everything was okay from the faith cure.

MRS. BITTNER: Could you give me in a general way, Mr. Coryer, a little bit more background to this faith cure, something about . . . the rules of this cure and something about the people themselves?

MR. CORYER: Well, this faith cure couldn't be handed down to most anyone. It had to be a man of good character and not a man that was addicted to drinking very much. Of course, they could take a drink, but not get drunk and get out of their minds so's that they would use this when they shouldn't use it, and also abuse the use of this prayer, this cure. And they could teach only three. Each man that knew this could teach three others, and no more, before their death.

And of course, the different generations was first, as I said, Mr. Limery that brought this here. He was one of the first settlers at Frenchtown. And then he taught it to Mr. Basil Gagnier. And then Mr. Gagnier taught Mr. Joseph LaRock and Charles Valley. And then Mr. Charles Valley taught his son, Joe Valley, and also taught myself, Albert Coryer, and then I taught the two grandsons of Mr. Valley, the man that taught me the same thing, and they are the last ones that have been taught this from Mr. Valley. Mr. LaRock taught William Valley and also Albert LaBonne. Albert LaBonne is still living in Prairie du Chien. And that is the way this prayer has been handed down, this cure has been handed down. But of late it's not used so much because the doctors are available any time that anyone has anything go wrong about them and they need help, of course they run to doctors and don't make use of this cure very much. But years ago when doctors weren't available and . . . people would have died, they were glad to have this cure administered to them, and it has cured and helped many.

Now this cure isn't only for rattlesnake bites, but such as eczema, rashes, or other ailments similar to that, and the healer is not supposed to collect or expect any money as a payment. They're not supposed to make a money racket of this. Or it's not a moneymaking concern at all. You're not supposed to use it for making money. It has been proven that where the man that said the prayers or did the healing has accepted or asked for pay, the cure didn't affect the one that was being doctored.

A TRUE GHOST STORY

Written by Albert Coryer, grandson of Mr. Thaddeus Langford and his wife, Eliza, nee Eliza Hutchinson.

Thaddeus was born in Troy, New York, about the year 1810, and Eliza was born in Montreal, Canada. She was a few years younger than her husband. Thaddeus left home at the age of twelve and worked his way to Milwaukee, Wisconsin. There he got a job as an engineer in a flour mill. He had not been there long when he met his wife, Eliza. Eliza had emigrated from Canada to Milwaukee, Wisconsin, with her parents and two sisters.

Now Thaddeus and Eliza met and after some time of courtship, they were married. They lived in Milwaukee a few years, and a daughter was born to them. Malvina was born in a frame house, which stood where the Milwaukee Depot now is. The house was moved away to make room for the depot. [Malvina] was born February 2, 1847. When she was three years of age, Thaddeus was transferred from Milwaukee to Chicago to engineer a new [flour] mill the company had built there.

Of course, the first thing to do when they reached Chicago was to locate a place to live. As Thaddeus had a partner to work with him, a man named Brown with a family of children, they wanted to rent a house large enough for two families and located near their work. On inquiring, all they could get to rent was a large apartment house only partly finished inside and owned by the city. The city had gotten the building through taxes. When Thaddeus and Brown met the city officials and spoke to them as to their living in this house, the officials told them that one end of the building was finished with room for one family [on] the first floor and the other on the second floor. On asking the officials how much rent they wanted for the rooms, the officials answered, "We ask no rent because the house is haunted and several families have gotten out of it badly frightened."

And Thaddeus laughed and said, "Okay, we will try it."

Thaddeus and Brown did not believe in this haunted affair and made it up not to let their wives know of what was told to them by the city officials.

So they moved in; the Brown family occupied the first floor because they had three children and Mrs. Brown was sort of a delicate woman, and [the] Langfords moved in the upstairs rooms. Mrs. Langford was strong and had only one daughter, Malvina.

Everything was just okay for about a week. Then one morning, about eleven o'clock, Eliza was startled by hearing a crash which sounded as if Mrs. Brown's dish cupboard had toppled over and many dishes were broken. So she hurriedly went downstairs to console Mrs. Brown. As she was about to descend the stairs, she met Mrs. Brown, [who] was about to come upstairs to see what had happened to Eliza's dish cupboard because the crash sounded to her to be upstairs.

On meeting in the stairs, they argued as to where the crash was, so Eliza said, "I won't be satisfied until I see that your dish cupboard is okay." So, they both went down to Mrs. Brown's cupboard and realized it was okay. Then they went up to Eliza's cupboard and found it had not toppled over.

Now this put a bug in the women's head that something spooky had happened.

The men worked twelve-hour shifts, so one of them was sleeping and the other was working at the mill.

As soon as the women could get to tell their husbands of the spooky affair, they told them. But the men just laughed it off and said that's like women imagining things.

About a week later, Thaddeus was home nights and worked day shift. Their bedroom was at the top of the stairs, with a short corridor from stairs to the bedroom. This room was a corner room, and the streetlight shone through the windows as to make it quite light. As to their house lights, all they had was candles, and the old sulfur matches, which were slow to ignite.

Well, Thaddeus and Eliza had gone to bed. Thaddeus was tired and had fallen asleep when Eliza heard a man's footsteps coming up the stairs. Her first thoughts were—did we forget to lock the door at the foot of the stairs. Then she thought it must be Brown coming to get Thaddeus. Something must have gone wrong at the mill. So she awakened Thaddeus.

Thaddeus quickly got up and as he did so, the man's footsteps had reached the top of the stairs. Apparently, the man fell backwards down the stairs by the sound. The body rolled to the bottom of the stairs, and the man moaned and groaned as if badly injured. Thaddeus told Eliza to light the candle, and he quickly made his way to the bottom of the stairs saying, "Are you hurt badly, Brown?" But no answer came. On reaching the stair landing, he reached about for Brown, but he found nothing there. By this time Eliza had come with the candle and nothing could be seen. So Eliza said, "Try the door. He may have escaped before you got here." On trying the door, they found it locked.

Then Eliza said, "Now do you think us women imagine things?" Thaddeus said nothing as the city official's statement came to his mind. But this got the strong and fearless Thaddeus to thinking such things can happen.

They went to bed but did not get to sleep for some time thinking of the mystery.

Well, everything was quiet for a few days, and the shock had been about forgotten when Thaddeus and Eliza had just got to bed. Neither of them were asleep, and the same sound of footsteps up the stairs, "thump-thump," were heard by both. So Thaddeus said to Eliza, "I'll get the rascal this time." So Thaddeus went to the door that led to the stairs, and as he was about to pounce at the offender at the stair top, the man fell backwards "apparently" downstairs. So Thaddeus hurried and said, "I'll get you this time, you rascal." The same groaning was heard as it was heard the time previous. Thaddeus reached the landing, and the groaning was still heard near him. Thaddeus said, "Groan if you will. I'll get you."

Eliza came with the candle. Nothing was to be seen, and the door at the foot of [the] stairs was locked. Again, Eliza said, "It is strange us women imagine things." But Thaddeus still held his nerve and thought it was tricks someone was doing, so he just said that he was not going out for this nonsense. So he told Eliza, "If it ever happened that those footsteps were heard again, we will just let it go on, and we will not get excited and see what will happen."

So, a week or longer time passed, and as usual shortly after retiring, and they were both still awake, the same "thump-thump" was heard up the stairs. But this time the footsteps came to the door. As the light from the street made it quite light, [as] the steps came to the door, Thaddeus got up and stood by the bed. To their astonishment, a man appeared in the door and put a hand on each side of the door frame and looked their way. Eliza and Thaddeus both took close notice of his appearance. He was a medium-sized man, dressed as the Scotchmen dressed at that time. [He wore] a Scotch cap and knee-length trousers with long stockings up to [the] trousers and strap above the knee.

Now that Thaddeus had taken close observance of the whole affair, he made a lunge at the Scotchman. But before he could reach the door where he stood, Thaddeus heard the same "rump a ty bump" down the stairs and the same moaning. Thaddeus was sure he had him this time and hurried to the stair landing and as usual found nothing. This conquered the strong and fearless Thaddeus, and he said to Eliza, "We are moving out of here as soon as possible. This is enough. Something has happened in this building, and I am going to find out what did happen."

PART II

They found a house to move in; it was not so convenient to their place of employment or living conditions, but at that [place,] they were not disturbed by the Scotchman's ghost.

Now Thaddeus had, or rather was determined, to solve the mystery. So he went to the city officials and told them the whole story and admitted he had been driven out by the ghostly nuisance.

At this in turn, the officials laughed and said, "You told us an old story."

So Thaddeus asked the officials if they would permit him to search and investigate to find out the cause of this mystery. The officials gladly gave him permission to investigate.

The first thing he did was he asked the officials how the city had gotten the building and who had built it and owned it to begin with.

NOW THE STORY OF THE SCOTCHMAN

A Scotchman, a stranger and alone, came to [Chicago], apparently with much money, with the intention of building an apartment house. He bought the lot to build on. He was talented as to building; he did all his planning and hired carpenters and told them what to do. He was on the job before others at any time and apparently had plenty of money to carry on with the project.

The Scotchman lived with another family who lived just across the street from his building. [One] morning the men working for him had all [arrived] ready to work. The boss or Scotchman was not there, as he usually was there first. They knew that the work had to be done as was told them, so they worked on as usual. The day passed and no Scotchman came, so they decided it would be their duty to go to his rooming house and investigate. On asking, the lady of the house told them that the Scotchman had left for Scotland to get more money to finish the building. He told her to tell them to continue with the work until they ran out of material to work with and then wait until he got back.

This sounded strange to the carpenters because the man had always been honest and outright with them. Why should he go and not tell them of it. Not many days after, the family the Scotchman lived with disappeared, and no one knew where they went to. And the Scotchman never came back.

Time went on, and no one paid taxes on the building, so the city took it over for back taxes. Therefore, the Scotchman had been murdered, and his body had been disposed of in an unknown way.

By inquiring in different angles, Thaddeus got to thinking. It came to his mind he should make a thorough investigation of the building where the Scotchman was still active in a ghostly form. Now, this building had a full basement and no floor in the basement, just sand. So it came to Thaddeus to have a few rods of steel about six feet long and sharp at one end made by a blacksmith. And then he invited as many men as he had rods to come with him to the basement. They used those rods by driving them down in the sand, not missing a square foot of space. By so doing, one of the men struck something about two feet from the surface. The men all stopped, and one dug down to where the object was. They found a lime barrel buried there. They got the barrel out and opened it, and they found the body of the Scotchman crumbled in the barrel. He was dressed with the same clothing to that which Thaddeus and others had seen him in his ghostly appearances.

The city officials had that which remained of him [placed] in a coffin and buried the remains in a cemetery. This ended the ghostly appearances and strange sounds in the building, which the Scotchman had built.

This story was told to me by my mother, which was Malvina Langford, and her two brothers, Orville and Eugene Langford, children of Thaddeus and Eliza Langford.

Thaddeus and Eliza told their children in a sober and truthful way that it really had happened. Then my mother and my uncles told me as it was told them. Thereby, it must be a true ghost story.

Yours Truly,

Albert E. Coryer

THIS IS NOT A GHOST STORY BUT A STRANGE INCIDENT

Thaddeus left Chicago in the year 1854 and moved to the township of Eastman in the County of Crawford. He bought forty acres of land three miles east of the corners on Shanghai Ridge.

At this date there was no sign of a village where the village of Eastman now is. When two old settlers wanted to mention the spot, they called it the corners because of the road from Lynxville to Steuben crossed the Black River road which is now Highway 27. And as [one of] the old settlers, Thaddeus kept busy in the timber, splitting rails for fencing and logs for buildings.

Of course, a forty-acre [piece] of land is one-quarter mile square, so at all times he was not far from his log hut where his wife was. When mealtime came about, Eliza would call him.

One morning as he was working as usual, he heard a woman's voice call him. T-h-a-d-d-e-u-s. By the sound, he could not determine what direction [the call] came from, and the voice was not Eliza's voice. So, he decided to disregard the affair and went back to work. The call came a second time. He could not determine what direction the call came from. So he went to work again, trying to determine whose voice it was calling him. Finally, when he heard the call for the third time, he started for home. On entering the house, Eliza asked him what had happened, and then he told her of hearing the call three times and that he made up his mind it was her calling. She answered, "No, I did not call. It is only eleven o'clock."

At that time, there were not railroads coming or going in Prairie [du Chien], and it took about three weeks for mail to travel from New York State to Prairie by boats and stages drawn by horses, with just trails for roads. So, about three weeks after Thaddeus heard the strange calling, he received a letter from Troy, New York, with the sad news that his mother had died just about the day he heard the call in the woods.

ANOTHER STRANGE STORY: BELIEVE IT OR NOT BY ALBERT CORYER

It was a nice still morning in the early part of the summer. Julian Coryer had gone to work in his field. His wife, Lucretia, took care of the morning work about the house, and then she went to her garden to work there. The garden spot was not far from the house, so she left her son, Joseph, sleeping. Joseph at this time [1851] was about six years of age.

Sometime after Lucretia went to the garden, Joseph awoke. As he realized his mother was in the garden, he went there and asked her for his breakfast.

Lucretia was interested in her work, so she told Joseph to go to the kitchen where he would find food. So Joseph started back. To get to the kitchen, he had to pass by the dining room. As he passed by a window, his sight was attracted to the window. On looking well, he saw a woman sitting in a position so that he was looking at her side. She sat there motionless. So Joseph took a good look at her to see if he knew her, but he soon realized he did not know her. He hurried to his mother in the garden and told her about seeing the strange woman.

Lucretia dropped her hoe and hurried to the house. Joseph told her where to look so she would see the woman; but there was no woman there. So Lucretia hurried around the house on the outside, thinking the woman had got tired waiting and had left. Now the distance from the house to the garden [is such that] the woman could have never gotten out of sight. [Lucretia] saw no one, so she hurried about inside the house. No one could be seen there. So she got impatient and said to Joseph, "You are lying to me, are you not." Joseph felt bad and said, "No, I am not lying." Then Lucretia asked him to tell her what color the woman's dress was. He told her she wore a light brown dress with white dots in it, and she wore a black shoulder shawl as most women wore in those days.

So Lucretia said, "I'll tell your father when he comes at noon." Joseph started crying and said, "Tell him if you care to. I saw the woman in the window as I told you."

So Lucretia gave Joseph food and returned to work in the garden. Noontime came about and Julian came in to eat his meal. Lucretia told him this way. "What do you think, Julian? Our son lied to me this morning." Joseph felt offended and said, "I was not lying. I really saw a woman in the window." Lucretia told Joseph to describe the woman as he saw her, so he did. He described her exactly as he did to his mother in the morning.

After listening to Joseph's description, [Julian] said, "He saw Aunt Elsie as I saw her for the last time in Canada." Well, the mystery had been about forgotten. Julian went to the post office. He received a letter with the sad news in it that his Aunt Elsie had died, and as they wrote the day of her death, it was the day Joseph saw the strange woman in the window.

Now why I remembered and believed those stories told by my parents is that I never caught my father or mother lying to me.

And my parents said the same of their parents.

Therefore, believe it or not. Not by Ripley: but by Albert Coryer.

Appendix: Frenchtown School as Remembered by Albert Coryer

The first schoolhouse built in Frenchtown was built on a plot of land one hundred feet square on the northeast corner of Joseph Gremore's little farm, which is now owned by John Sawvell. It was built about the year 1857 or 1859.

As I understand the first teacher was Theophile Dame, a man very strict and [who] punished [his students] severely.

The scholars at that time were Orlean Saul Washington, Fred Stram, Oliver and John Gremore, the Gagniers, the Gardipis, the Merciers, the La Pointes, and also Robert, Charles, and Frank Gremore.

I, Albert Coryer, started going to school in this schoolhouse, known as school of District No. 9 in town of Prairie du Chien. In fall of 1885, Miss Alice Nugent of 4th ward Prairie du Chien [was the teacher]. Next was Kate Duffy of 4th ward Prairie du Chien. Next was Miss Olive Sherwood of Mt. Sterling. Next was Dollie Calloway of Boscobel, Wisconsin. Next was Pearl Dietrich of 4th ward, who was my last teacher.

After those [women] were Miss Nelda Bosch of Prairie, but the next one I cannot remember [her] name. Next was Eva Chase of Prairie du Chien and [finally] was Maggie Sweeney of McGregor, Iowa. This is the last of teachers in [the] old school. Now, the new school [was] built about the year 1900. The first teacher [was] Anna Garrity of Prairie du Chien, then a Miss Foley of Prairie du Chien, then Miss Irene Valley of Frenchtown, and then Isolin Brookover from Wauzeka, Wisconsin.

Then the district decided it would be more economical and better to transport children to city schools.

Those who went to Frenchtown School starting the fall of 1885 were:

The Coryers—Albert, Della, and George

The Langfords—Orville, Myrtle, Bernice, and Thaddeus

The Gokeys—Rosina, Edward, Mary, Tilda, Helen, Frank, Peter, and Jane

The Gremores—Emily and Madeline

The Strams—August, Mayme, Roman, Tina, Frank, Fred, Clement, and Clara

The Cherriers—Walter, Irene, Willa, LeRoy, and Raymond

The Cayas—but cannot remember the first name

The La Pointes—Louis and Anthony

The Wachters—Lillie, Mattie, Herman, Emma, John, and Casper

The Ahrens—Fred, Minnie, and Ida

The Feidlers "Emmigrants"—Herman and Anna

The Huberts—Herbert

The Valleys—Emery and Felix

The Howes—Harry

The Kasts—May, Henry and Westley

The Emersons—Mayme and Myrtle

The Swingles—Walter

The Konneckecks [Konichek]—Charles Anthony, Edward, Frank and George

The Buschs—Theresa, Martha, Luther and Anna

The Scherlins—Fred

The La Voies—Nettie

The La Bonnes—Carrie and Edith

The Smalls—Loren and Earl

The Valleys—Evalyn, Irene, Delia, Agnes and two sons and two other girls.

The Mapson girls

And several others I cannot name.

Notes

Introduction

1. Helen Hornbeck Tanner, *Atlas of Great Lakes Indian History* (Norman, OK: University of Oklahoma Press, 1987), 42; for an in-depth discussion of this early history, see Lucy Eldersveld Murphy, *A Gathering of Rivers: Indians, Métis, and Mining in the Western Great Lakes, 1737–1832* (Lincoln: University of Nebraska Press, 2000), chapters 1–2. Also, Jonathan Carver was told in 1766 that the Meskwakis had moved to Prairie du Chien thirty years earlier; *Jonathan Carver's Travels through America, 1766–1768* [1788] (New York: Wiley, 1993), 75.

2. For more information about the history of Prairie du Chien, see Mary Elise Antoine, *Prairie du Chien* (Charleston, SC: Arcadia, 2011); Lucy Eldersveld Murphy, *Great Lakes Creoles: A French-Indian Community on the Northern Borderlands, Prairie du Chien, 1750–1860* (New York: Cambridge University Press, 2014); Peter L. Scanlan, *Prairie du Chien: French, British, American* (Appleton, WI: George Banta, 1937).

3. Jacqueline Peterson, "The People in Between: Indian-White Marriage and the Genesis of a Métis Society and Culture in the Great Lakes Region, 1680–1830," PhD diss., University of Illinois at Chicago Circle, 1981.

4. Carver actually called it both "La Prairie le Chien" and "La Praires les Chiens which signifies the Dog Plains" (*Jonathan Carver's Travels*, 60, 76). Peter Pond called it "Planes (sic) of the Dogs" (Charles M. Gates, *Five Fur Traders of the Northwest* [St. Paul: Minnesota Historical Society Press, 2014], 44; Elliott Coues, ed., *The Expeditions of Zebulon Montgomery Pike* [New York: Dover, 1987], 303).

5. Coues, ed., *The Expeditions of Zebulon Montgomery Pike*, 1:303–305.

6. James L. Hansen, "The Pelletier dit Antaya Families of Prairie du Chien," *The Genealogist* (forthcoming).

7. By 1850, two-thirds of the Creole men were farmers, according to the US census.

8. Mary Agnes Starr, *Pea Soup and Johnny Cake* (Madison, WI: Red Mountain, 1981), 45; Mary Elise Antoine interview with Donna Gokey, June 28, 2015.

Part 1

1. William G. Mosier was born in about 1800. He is in the 1870 Federal Census, living on the south end of the prairie. By 1880, he was in Richland County. He had a sizable farm, a flouring mill, and a sawmill.

2. Joseph Drew (1818–1901) was the son of an enlisted man who had been stationed at Fort Crawford in Prairie du Chien and then Fort Snelling. After his father's death, Joseph and his younger brother David returned to Prairie du Chien and were living on the prairie by 1837. Joseph made a living farming for others. Beginning in the 1870s, he was employed as a servant in the Dousman household.

3. The previous two sentences are from the Bittner interview.

4. This paragraph and the next one were moved from the end of this manuscript to here, where the events fit chronologically.

5. The previous sentence is from the Bittner voyageur manuscript.

6. The previous four sentences are from the Bittner voyageur manuscript.

7. The previous four sentences are from the Bittner voyageur manuscript.

8. Native Americans had used fire to modify their environment for thousands of years to create both cleared areas good for farming and relatively open forests better for hunting and traveling. Coryer's comments reveal that the Creole residents also used fire to modify the landscape.

9. Barbed wire, developed in DeKalb, Illinois, became commercially available in 1874.

10. For centuries, Native people had made sugar in regions where the sugar maple grew. European traders introduced kettles as trade goods, a technology that improved the sugar-making process considerably. Indian women were generally in charge of the sugar groves and managed the process. Native people taught the newcomers how to make sugar. Because there was extensive intermarriage between Native women and French men, often this knowledge was passed from Indian mothers to their mixed-heritage children.

11. The previous five sentences are from the Bittner voyageur manuscript.

12. Hercules L. Dousman (1800–1868) came to Prairie du Chien as a clerk for the American Fur Company and worked for Joseph Rolette, an independent fur trader. In 1834, with the reorganization of the American Fur Company, Dousman, Rolette, and Henry Sibley formed the Western Outfit that operated in the upper Mississippi River Valley. Through the fur trade,

Dousman formed many business and political connections and began to invest in real estate, lumbering mills, and steamboats. In 1852, Dousman became the largest shareholder in the newly chartered Madison and Prairie du Chien Railroad. By 1860, Dousman was a man of wealth and influence. He established an estate in Prairie du Chien. In 1868, his son Louis inherited the estate. He dismantled the original family house and constructed a new home. After Louis's death in 1886, his widow, Nina, named the family property "Villa Louis."

13. William G. Mosier appears in the 1860 census of Linton Township, Allamakee County, Iowa, a miller, born in New York in 1821.

14. This sentence is from the interview.

15. The previous sentence is from the Bittner interview.

16. This paragraph is from the Bittner interview.

17. This paragraph is from the Bittner interview.

18. This paragraph is from the Bittner interview.

19. This paragraph is from the Bittner interview.

20. This paragraph is from "The Life of Julian Coryer."

21. The mysterious lights called will o' the wisp, also known as ghost-light or *ignis fatuus*, is a phenomenon mentioned in the folklore of Europe and the United States for many centuries. One explanation that has been offered for the lights, often seen in swampy areas at night, is that they might be caused by phosphine, volatile gases. Joris Roels and Willy Verstraete, "Biological Formation of Volatile Phosphorus Compounds," *Bioresource Technology* 79, no. 3 (September 2001), 243–250.

22. Marie Carriere was baptized on November 30, 1856, at St. Gabriel's Church in Prairie du Chien. According to the church record, she was about six years of age. Where her parents should have been listed, it states, "Unknown taken from the Indians and given above Name." Original page 127, entry #107, found in transcript, Peter L. Scanlan, "Registre de Catholicite de la Prairie du Chien, 1840–," Wisconsin Historical Society, Platteville Mss D, Box 7, Folder 3, 75.

23. In 1870, Louis Dousman contracted with E. Townsend Mix to construct a new home on the site of the "House on the Mound," which Hercules Dousman had had erected in 1843. The new house was completed in 1871. The name "Villa Louis" was not given to the property until after Louis's death in 1886.

24. Adelaide Gagnier Limery (1802–1860) was the daughter of Claude Gagnier and Marianne Labuche. Marianne, an Afro-French woman from New Orleans, was revered throughout the community for her knowledge of medicinal herbs. Adelaide probably learned her skills not only from Native healers but also from her mother. Adelaide married Jean Baptiste L'Emerie (Limery). The couple lived along a stream that flowed from a coulee to the Mississippi River. The coulee came to be called Limery, and the Carriere/Coryer family farmed to the north of Limery Coulee.

25. American spikenard is a perennial herbaceous plant growing three to five feet tall. The Micmac Indians used the root of the spikenard to heal wounds and cuts, while the Ojibwe used the root as a poultice to heal fractured bones.

26. None of these buildings is extant as of 2015.

Part 2

1. Giacomo Constantino Beltrami, *A Pilgrimage in Europe and America* (London: Hunt & Clarke, 1828), 2:174.

2. Henry R. Schoolcraft, *A View of the Lead Mines of Missouri* (New York: Charles Wiley, 1819), 39.

3. "Local Business," *Crawford County Courier*, Prairie du Chien, May 17, 1853, 2.

4. Campbell Coulee later became known as Ahrens Coulee and Cliffwood Drive.

5. Visits by priests were sporadic before 1827, a bit more frequent during the 1830s, and then in 1840 the first pastor, Father Augustin Ravoux, arrived.

6. The Chicago, Burlington and Quincy Railroad came to Prairie du Chien in 1888.

7. Mary Lessard (Marie Rose Bastian Lessard, 1782–1869) was listed in the 1860 federal census as age seventy-seven. She lived with John Lessard, age twenty-nine, next door to Joseph and Monique Lessard and family, and to Leander and Victoria Lessard and family. All of the men were listed as farmers.

8. The Jeandron family appears in the list of the children of Sauk and/or Meskwaki mothers and Euro-American fathers. Pierre Jeandron and Kayawiscoquoi were the parents of Pierre, fils, who was born about 1809

(Thomas Forsyth Papers, Lyman Draper Manuscripts, microfilm, 2T 22, Wisconsin Historical Society Archives).

9. Moses Caya appears in the 1850 US census as age twenty-five, a farmer, born in Canada with a wife, Mary, age nineteen, born in Wisconsin, and son Joseph, age two, also born in Wisconsin. The house in which the Moses Caya family lived is listed in the National Register of Historic Places. It is the Francois Vertefeuille House and was built in the French-Canadian method of *pièce sur pièce en coulisse*. Moses purchased the house in 1854.

10. Alex Chenevert appears in the 1860 US census as age forty-one, born in Wisconsin, a farmer, with wife Cinde, age thirty-five, also born in Wisconsin. Nicholas Chenevert (1811–1892), in 1860, was thirty-nine years old, a farmer, with wife Mary, age thirty-three.

11. The 1850 census lists Alexis Gardipie, born in 1812 in Canada, a farmer; and his wife, Angelic (nee Desilait), born in Canada in the same year. Their children were Charles, Victoria, and Frank, ages eleven, eight, and one.

12. Coryer's map calls this man Fred Lapointe. In the 1850 census, Fred was listed as age two, the son of Bartelmy, age forty, and Victoria (nee Plante), age forty. John Lapointe was fifteen years old in 1850, living with Oliver Cherrier's family.

13. In 1850, the census taker noted both Michael and Joseph Godfrey, age thirty-five and forty, respectively, born in Canada, living with Louis Laforce and "chopping wood" for a living.

14. In 1860, Joseph and Mary Booth, ages sixty-three and forty-two, farmed and had Thomas Booth, age twenty-eight, and Adelia, age nineteen, living with them. All four were listed as having been born in Canada.

15. In the 1860 census, farmer Louis Cayay [sic], age forty-six, born in Canada, was listed living with wife Adelia, age thirty-two, born in Wisconsin, and six children. They lived next to the Booths.

16. In 1860, Oliver Grimard (1838–1911) was a twenty-one-year-old day laborer, living with his parents, Peter (Pierre) and Elizabeth. His mother's maiden name was Courtois.

17. In 1860, Louis Stram (1808–1886), born in Switzerland, ran a grocery and provisioning business with his wife, Julia Catherine, who had been born in Missouri. In the same year Augustus Stram, a thirty-four-year-old farmer born in Red River of the North, and his Wisconsin-born wife,

Margaret (nee Hebert), were living with Margaret and Richard Price, ages twenty-four and twenty-seven, respectively. Margaret Stram was the daughter of Augustus Hebert dit LeBlanc (b. 1777, d. November 30, 1828) and Cheenawpaukie, a Meskwaki woman. Information on Margaret Hebert Price Stram from St. Gabriel's Church record, p. 14 of Scanlan typescript. Les and Jeanne Rentmeester, *Wisconsin Creoles*, gives her date of birth as 1815, p. 272; James L. Hansen, "Prairie du Chien's Earliest Church Records, 1817," *Minnesota Genealogical Journal*: 4 (November 1985), 10; Thomas Forsyth Papers, Lyman Draper Manuscripts, microfilm, 2T 22, Wisconsin Historical Society; Thomas Forsyth, Records of the Superintendent of Indian Affairs, St. Louis, Kansas State Historical Society, vol. 32, "Sac-Fox 1/2 Breeds."

18. John Limery is Jean Baptiste L'Emerie (1768–1846), born in Quebec. The name was Anglicized to Limery. Jean Baptiste and Adelaide Gagnier had a son, John, born in Prairie du Chien in 1828.

19. Oliver Cherrier appeared in the 1860 census, age forty-four, as a prosperous farmer born in Wisconsin, with wife Madeline, seven children, a child with a different surname, and a male domestic worker, born in France. Everyone else in the household was born in Wisconsin.

20. According to the 1860 census, Joseph Grimard (1835–1917), age twenty-four, was a farmer living with his wife, Elizabeth (nee Plante). They had two small children named Elizabeth and Rose, and a fourteen-year-old servant girl, Frances LaPointe, living with them. All had been born in Wisconsin. Next door was Peter (Pierre) Grimard (1796–1860), age sixty-two, a farmer born in Canada; wife Elizabeth, born in Wisconsin; son Oliver, age twenty-one; four teenagers; and two infants.

21. The lake is called Gremore Lake, an Anglicized version of Grimard.

22. For much of the nineteenth century, the property of wives came under the control of their husbands.

23. In the 1850 census, Charles Courtois was living in the household of Peter Grimard and his wife, Elisabeth, whose maiden name was Courtois.

24. Charles Menard (1807–unknown) and his wife, Frances [nee Hebert], ages fifty-two and forty-five, appeared in the 1860 census, living near his brother Pascal Menard (c.1813–1882) and Pascal's wife, Mary, ages forty-five and thirty-six, and their four children. Both men listed their occupations as farming.

25. In the 1860 census, Bazile Gagnier (c. 1802–1878), age fifty-seven, and his wife, Josephine, age fifty-two, were farming. They had two children at home; three older children listed in the 1850 census had apparently moved out to establish their own households.

26. From the 1860 census, Theodore "Legro" Chenevert (1810–1883), age fifty, a farmer, was born in Canada. His wife was Mary, age thirty-six, and they had a ten-month-old baby, also named Mary. His nickname probably came from the French "le gros," meaning "the big," to distinguish him from his son, Theodore, born in 1862.

Part 3

1. For more information, see Carolyn Podruchny, *Making the Voyageur World: Travelers and Traders in the North American Fur Trade* (Lincoln: University of Nebraska Press, 2006).

2. Quebec, Vital and Church Records (Drouin Collection), 1621–1967 (online database), http://search.ancestry.com/search/db.aspx?dbid=1091.

3. Voyageur database, Centre du patrimonie, Société historique de Saint-Boniface, www.voyageurs.shsh.mb.ca.

4. General Land Office Records, Bureau of Land Management, US Department of the Interior, Accession #MW-0176-008, Military Warrant, Wisconsin, August 12, 1858, www.glorecords.blm.gov.

5. Isaac H. Elliot, *Record of the Services of Illinois Soldiers in the Black Hawk War, 1831–32, and in the Mexican War, 1846–8* (Springfield, IL: H. W. Rokker, 1882), 142–143.

6. Missouri, Marriage Records, 1805–2002 (online database). Ancestry.com.

7. Papers of the St. Louis Fur Trade, part 2, microfilm reel #6, ledger book X; and microfilm reel #7, ledger book AA, Missouri Historical Society, St. Louis, Missouri.

8. 1840 United States Federal Census (online database), Ancestry.com.

9. Wisconsin, Compiled Census and Census Substitutes Index, 1820–1890 (online database), Ancestry.com.

10. 1850 United States Federal Census (online database), Ancestry.com.

11. Papers of the St. Louis Fur Trade, part 2, microfilm reel #6, ledger book X; and microfilm reel #7, ledger book AA, Missouri Historical Society, St. Louis, Missouri.

12. Julian Carriere was baptized on June 13, 1813, in the church of Saint

Marguerite-de-Blairfindie in the village of l'Acadie. As Albert stated in his interview with Mrs. Bittner, his family had originally settled in Acadia and had been part of the diaspora. This causes some confusion when Albert states "La Bay du Fave" was Julian's birthplace. A Baie-du-Febvre is located between Trois-Rivieres and Sorel, a distance northeast of l'Acadie.

13. This sentence was added from the Bittner voyageur manuscript.

14. This sentence was added from the Bittner voyageur manuscript.

15. This sentence was added from the Bittner voyageur manuscript.

16. This sentence was added from the Bittner voyageur manuscript.

17. According to the Bittner voyageur manuscript, they were headed to Green Bay.

18. According to the Bittner voyageur manuscript, the holes were patched with leather.

19. This sentence was added from the Bittner voyageur manuscript.

20. The woman Julian remembered is Elizabeth Pelletier dit Antaya. She married Jean Marie Cardinal. Jean Marie was buried April 30, 1832, at Prairie du Chien. Elizabeth is not listed in the 1830 federal census.

21. The population of Prairie du Chien in 1830, excluding the soldiers and families stationed at Fort Crawford, was 363.

22. The previous two paragraphs are from the Bittner interview.

23. This sentence is from the Bittner voyageur manuscript.

24. According to the Bittner voyageur manuscript, the merchandise included blankets, rifles, ammunition, tobacco, alcohol, beads, needles and thread, salt, and paints such as vermillion.

25. Coryer was probably referring to keelboats, which were used extensively on the Mississippi and Missouri Rivers to transport goods. Until 1830, the keelboat was the only means to move goods up the Missouri River to the trading posts built by the American Fur Company and continued to be used for several years beyond that.

26. The previous four sentences are from the Bittner voyageur manuscript.

27. The post was probably Fort Union, commanded by Kenneth McKenzie. Fort Union was "the central and principal depot for all the trade of the upper country" (Barton H. Barbour, *Fort Union and the Upper Missouri Fur Trade* [Norman: University of Oklahoma Press, 2002], 40–43).

28. The previous five sentences are from the Bittner voyageur manuscript.

29. This sentence is from the Bittner voyageur manuscript.

30. This sentence is from the Bittner voyageur manuscript.

31. This sentence is from the Bittner voyageur manuscript.

32. The previous two sentences are from the Bittner voyageur manuscript.

33. Minor details in this paragraph were added from the Bittner voyageur manuscript.

34. Minor details in this paragraph were added from the Bittner voyageur manuscript.

35. This sentence was added from the Bittner voyageur manuscript.

36. The amount was a cord per man per day, according to the Bittner voyageur manuscript.

37. In the Bittner voyageur manuscript, Coryer said, "Julian had a better eye to spy the game."

38. In the Bittner voyageur manuscript, they verbally accused each other of using too much salt.

39. Minor details in this paragraph were added from the Bittner voyageur manuscript.

40. Minor details in this paragraph have been added from the Bittner voyageur manuscript.

41. According to the Bittner voyageur manuscript, they were hobbled "with a strong leather strap of about a foot long connected to two hobble straps."

42. Minor details in this paragraph have been added from the Bittner voyageur manuscript.

43. Minor details have been added to this paragraph from the Bittner voyageur manuscript.

44. Minor details have been added to this paragraph from the Bittner voyageur manuscript.

45. Minor details in this paragraph were added from the Bittner voyageur manuscript.

46. Minor details in this paragraph were added from the Bittner voyageur manuscript.

47. Hiram Martin Chittenden, in *The American Fur Trade of the Far West*, vol. 1 (Lincoln: University of Nebraska Press, 1986), states that at Fort Union, Kenneth McKenzie's "discipline was severe, and he had little regard for human life when it stood in his way. He once offered to surrender to the merciless savages a man who had killed one of their number" (384). This story seems to indicate that Julian was present at the incident cited by Chittenden.

48. The previous two sentences are from the Bittner voyageur manuscript.

49. The previous three sentences are from the Bittner voyageur manuscript.

50. Some details in this paragraph were added from the Bittner voyageur manuscript.

51. Some details in this paragraph were added from the Bittner voyageur manuscript.

52. Some details in this paragraph were added from the Bittner voyageur manuscript.

53. Minor details in this paragraph have been added from the Bittner voyageur manuscript.

54. Minor details have been added to this paragraph from the Bittner voyageur manuscript.

55. This sentence is from the Bittner voyageur manuscript.

56. If an engagé fell ill, the American Fur Company still paid his wages and furnished him board and room. But the man had to pay for all of his medical expenses (Barton H. Barbour, *Fort Union and the Upper Missouri Fur Trade* [Norman: University of Oklahoma Press, 2002], 140).

57. Lucretia Lessard was the daughter of Jean Baptiste Lessard and Marie Rose Bastian. She was baptized April 20, 1819, in the church of St.-Antoine-de-Riviere-du-Loup in Louiseville, Quebec (Drouin Collection). The marriage of Julian and Lucretia was recorded as Julien Collier and Leocadie Lessart. They were married June 13, 1836, in St. Louis, Missouri (Missouri Marriage Records, 1805–2002).

58. Francois Gautier and Mary Anne Lessart were married April 20, 1835, by Joseph A. Lutz in St. Louis, Missouri (Drouin Collection).

59. The cholera epidemic affected St. Louis in 1832, 1833, 1835, and 1849. In the 1830s, more than 500 residents of St. Louis died, 1832 being the most virulent year. In 1849, the epidemic killed 6 percent of the population of St. Louis, more than 4,300 residents (Walter J. Daly, "The Black Cholera Comes to the Central Valley of American in the 19th Century—1832, 1849, and Later," *Transactions of the American Clinical and Climatological Associations* [2008]; 119:143–153).

60. Some details in this paragraph were added from the Bittner voyageur manuscript.

61. By 1842, Julian had moved to Wisconsin Territory. In that year, he was enumerated as living in Grant County (Wisconsin Census, 1820–1890).

62. Some details in this paragraph were added from the Bittner voyageur manuscript.

63. John and Frank Lessard were Jean Baptiste (born March 31, 1826) and Francois (born 1824), brothers of Lucretia and Mary Anne Lessard. Oliver Cherrier (born October 2, 1815) and Cosme Cherrier (born December 20, 1826) were both born in Prairie du Chien, the sons of Oliver Cherrier and Celeste Courtois. Mr. Rossou was Peter Rousseau (born in 1813).

64. Some details in this paragraph were added from the Bittner voyageur manuscript.

65. The route the Lessard brothers and their friends took to California was called the California Trail; it took people west from either Omaha, Nebraska, or Independence, Missouri, to California and the Oregon Territory. It took five to six months to complete the 2,400-mile journey. When gold was discovered in California, hundreds flooded the trail. For more information, see the National Park Service's page on the history of the California National Scenic Trail (www.nps.gov/cali/learn/historyculture/index.htm).

66. The Lessards and their fellow travelers would not have crossed Death Valley, California, on their way westward. The area Albert refers to in this story is along the Humboldt River called the Humboldt Sink, about one hundred miles (160 km) northeast of present-day Reno, Nevada.

67. Some details in this paragraph have been added from the Bittner voyageur manuscript.

68. According to the Bittner voyageur manuscript, they worked "on the docks at San Francisco, loading and unloading ships."

69. According to the Bittner voyageur manuscript, this farm was owned by Dan Swingle. Swingle was born in January 1889, son of William and Ida Swingle. He lived on the west side of Frenchtown Road and farmed the land east of the road.

70. Joseph Lessard was born August 25, 1821, in Canada. He married Monica Rosalie Limery on April 13, 1847, at St. Gabriel's Church, Prairie du Chien, Wisconsin. Monica, born in 1831, was the daughter of Jean Baptiste L'Emerie and Adelaide Gagnier.

71. Deeds filed at the Crawford County Register of Deeds do not bear out Albert's memories. His confusion may have been because two men, both with the first name Joseph, were involved in Julian's land dealings. On October

15, 1845, Julian Carriere sold to Joseph Trepagnier 69.9 acres of land "near Limery's Coulee." On January 25, 1848, Joseph and Monica Rosalie Lessard sold to Julian Carrier forty acres, with "all the Buildings, Fences and Other Improvements thereunto." As Joseph and Monica Lessard had been married less than a year, they did not have four children.

72. This sentence is from the Bittner voyageur manuscript.

73. This sentence is from the Bittner voyageur manuscript.

74. Ira Burr Brunson was the son of Rev. Alfred Brunson. Ira served in the Wisconsin Territorial legislature and was appointed postmaster at Prairie du Chien in 1840. Over the years, he held several Crawford County offices, including judge of probate court and surveyor. In 1856, he surveyed the Prairie du Chien Union Plat.

75. Coryer was referring to the Vallee and Proulx families, to whom Julian was related through his mother, Marie Caron. Henry Proulx (1831–1899) married Julia Vallee (1835–1910), the daughter of Antoine Vallee (1788–1881), and the family arrived in Prairie du Chien in 1852. Julian and Lucretia sold twenty acres of land to Henry Proulx.

76. Oliver Valley (1827–1918) purchased farmland adjacent to Frank Gokey. Olizeme Valley was a brother of Oliver.

Part 4

1. Owen Davies, "French Charmers and Their Healing Charms," in *Charms and Charming in Europe*, edited by Jonathan Roper (New York: Palgrave Macmillan, 2005), 91–104; Dana David, "A Vernacular Healing System: Reinventing the Circle with Cadien Treaters," unpublished paper, 2005, www.metanexus.net/archive/conference2005/pdf/david.pdf.

2. Mary Antoine correspondence with Patrick Brunet, April 22, 2015.

Acknowledgments

We are grateful for the help and support of the Wisconsin Historical Society Press and the cooperation of the Prairie du Chien Historical Society and Villa Louis historic site. All royalties will go to the latter two institutions. We would also like to thank Susan Leamy Kies for permission to use the materials from her collection and for sharing remembrances of Albert; Donna Higgins for permission to use material and images from her collection; Marie Gokey Ziel for making sure the manuscript of "Short Stories" was preserved; Janet Steele Lund for saving Vera Coryer's memories; and the Earl Valley family.

We appreciate how helpful James L. Hansen was in finding information about some of the people mentioned by Albert, and Rebecca Kugel for help with the Ojibwe language. Mary also would like to thank Patrick Brunet for sharing his memories of Albert and his information on "charmers," as well as Rita Gillitzer Lester for information on the Frenchtown School. We are also grateful to Michael Douglass for his encouragement and help with sources, and to Carolyn Podruchny and Ray DeMallie for comments about the voyageur stories. Lucy would like to thank former students Megan Cromwell, Alicia Barringer, Sande Garner, Hunter Garner, and Bryce Jones for typing, checking transcriptions, and other research assistance. The Ohio State University–Newark supported work on this project by funding student assistants and by granting a Scholarly Activity Grant, for which we are very grateful. And last but not least, we both give a great thank you to Erika Wittekind, our editor, for all her work and guidance.

About the Editors

Mary Elise Antoine, MA, is president of the Prairie du Chien Historical Society and former curator at Villa Louis. Her research focuses on the material culture and the mix and confrontation of cultures on the upper Mississippi prior to Wisconsin statehood. She is author of *The War of 1812 in Wisconsin*, also for the Wisconsin Historical Society Press, and two books on the history of Prairie du Chien.

Lucy Eldersveld Murphy, Ph.D., is a professor of history at the Ohio State University whose research focuses on intercultural, interracial, and gender relations on Midwestern American frontiers. She has written and edited four books and numerous articles and papers on Midwestern history.

Index